T0115163

Opening the Vault

A Personal Journey Through Autism & Schizophrenia

Is all that is mad insane?

by

Brigid Gallagher

BALBOA.
PRESS
A DIVISION OF HAY HOUSE

Balboa Press books may be ordered through booksellers or by contacting:

Balboa Press
A Division of Hay House
1663 Liberty Drive
Bloomington, IN 47403
www.balboapress.com.au
1-(877) 407-4847

ISBN: 978-1-4525-0627-2 (sc)
ISBN: 978-1-4525-0628-9 (e)

Printed in the United States of America

Balboa Press rev. date: 08/02/2012

This book is a testimonial to my son Michael, who showed me realities and truths I never knew existed and a peace and contentment I never imagined possible . . .

> *Come away O human child!*
> *To the waters and the wild*
> *with a faery hand in hand*
> *for the world's more full of weeping*
> *than you can understand.*

> ~ William Butler Yeats

I dedicate this book to Milica for believing in me and being my friend. Supported by her gentle encouragement, I found the courage to share Michael's remarkable story.

I am grateful to my dearest friend, my daughter Amelia-Jane, for her attention to detail, for staying and for being unshakable. It's a relief knowing that I didn't have to water this down to save her from the disturbing facts.

Warmest thanks, also, go to Rose and Jane, who read the first chapter and asked what happened next . . .

Table of Contents

Foreword

As so many great artists and visionaries have known—and as this inspiring book reminds us—soul is a bird which sings louder as the thorn is pressed to its breast. What you are about to read is an unashamedly honest, gutsy and emotionally intense journal of a family's shared travels through the tortuous but endlessly fascinating labyrinths of soul in crisis.

In my view, there are too few stories of this kind and calibre in print and, in contrast, too many clinical studies and theoretical treatises about autism and schizophrenia in the midst of which vibrant life tales like this are overshadowed by cold statistics and the debates of rival 'experts', many of whom have had no firsthand experience of intimately sharing the daily struggles of a loved one in the throes of a self-rebirthing ordeal. As well, the views, values, experience and insights offered by sufferers themselves are often dismissed as 'delusional' or 'paranoid' when ironically, as this uplifting and deeply moving book implies, they may be anything but. As the great physician of soul C. G. Jung made clear, we understand nothing psychologically unless we have experienced it.

Brigid Gallagher understands. She also has what it takes to gently capture the essence of her son Michael's ongoing and extraordinary journey: a rare passion, candidness, earthiness, soulfulness and exuberance for life. Above all, Brigid offers the non-judgmental acceptance, empathy, vulnerability and love which are indispensable qualities for anyone willing to help someone cope with the upheaval of a psychotic break from reality.

I've often felt that there is considerable overlap between autism and (what we call) schizophrenia. Many sufferers of both share a cluster of distinguishing traits: acute emotional sensitivity and empathy, a rich inner life, social withdrawal as an intense discomfort with loud social situations, eccentric genius, unpredictability and quirkiness, a childlike curiosity and need for wandering and exploration. In my own work with sufferers of schizophrenia, I have often been impressed and moved, too, by their inner beauty and shrewd insight into what ails our floundering world. From their perspective, it is the egocentricity, powermongering, lack of reverence for nature and crass materialism underpinning Western culture which is sick, manic and deluded and which has, in many instances, contributed to their breakdown. Thus they often become the scapegoats for a culture which remains blind to its lack of spiritual vision, destructive greed, insanity and loss of soul.

For genuine sufferers of schizophrenia, their crisis is a wound that often hides a great gift. Typically, it's a blessing and curse, a marriage of heaven and hell to those for whom it brings both anguish and revelation. It's also a kind of waking dream, where the archaic and often perilous world of myth, symbol, vision and religion displaces the world of mundane facts. And inevitably, as this book so beautifully portrays, its two-edged sword cuts deep into the soul of surrounding family life.

As I recall, the movie *A Beautiful Mind,* which portrayed the struggles of schizophrenic maths genius John Forbes Nash, focused—as this book does—on the power of unconditional and boundless love to transcend the psyche's wounds. Nash, like Michael, is a brilliant, unstable, introverted individual, whose disturbing behaviour and inner world of torment and vision is out of step with the status quo. What the film left out was that Nash (by his own accounts) stopped taking psychiatric drugs, learned to live with his 'voices' and—with the loving support of his wife—went on to win the Nobel Prize.

In other words, not all that is mad is insane; there is, rather, a kind of 'divine madness' that transcends the limits of reason, the five senses and cultural norms. Certainly all of Michael's visionary and auditory experiences—the voices, the Stephen King characters, encounters with aliens, guardian spirits and so on—at the very least have been real to him, and who is to say that he does not have access to realms of being that are closed to most of us? For folk like Michael, the veil between them and both the world and Otherworld realms of agony and ecstasy is extremely thin, or nonexistent, for better or worse, since dark and light, destructive and protective soul energies are often intertwined.

Interestingly, Michael's early fascination with caterpillars, alchemy and the transforming ocean hints at an instinctive foreseeing of his own metamorphosis—the breakdown that can lead to breakthrough and spiritual rebirth. When the crash does happen, he intuitively offsets his paralysing implosion by trying to impose order on the chaos, by inventing rules and routines as maternal vessels of containment and change. He is, in other words, an instinctive apprentice healer who understands soul's need to fragment, ritualise and return to calmly orbit its still centre.

At the end of the day, does Michael suffer from autism, or schizophrenia, or both? In the end, what do labels matter? The words 'schizophrenia' and 'autism' fail to do justice to the kaleidoscopic richness, vastness and inventiveness of the psyche and to the uniqueness of the individual. Michael comes across, rather, as enigmatic, special, surprising, delightful, bewildering, gifted, fragile as a soap bubble yet refracting life's vast colour spectrum like a diamond.

As World Health Organisation and other studies affirm, many people routinely recover from schizophrenia without any 'medical' intervention and, as this story illustrates, simply 'being there' for them in a caring home can provide the safe space in which the wounded psyche can restructure and heal itself. That Michael made it through the maze is testament not only to his instinct for truth and core strength but also to the psyche's uncanny ability to pull itself together after it has been shattered by life—and by the terrible and wondrous energies of the psychospiritual realm.

In stark contrast, the comparatively dull concept of 'mental illness' does not (also) exist as an objective medical fact; it exists, rather, purely in the eyes of a beholder who fails to understand what Buddhism teaches: that to be human is to suffer. What one person sees as an 'illness' or 'disorder' is often for the sufferer a potentially meaningful, sometimes shattering baptism and initiation into the boundless realms of soul. Psychiatric diagnostic labels, on the other hand, are mere inventions designed to categorise, medicalise, professionalise, depersonalise and foster the delusion that the sufferings of soul are abnormalities that can be explained as mere chemical imbalances in the brain. Meanwhile, the endlessly fascinating drama of the psyche as it is played out in the unique individual arena is all too often dismissed as 'illness'.

Again, Brigid understands by 'standing under' with open-hearted humility, instead of looking down from above in order to dominate, dissect, analyse, or control. She relates to Michael not as a problem to be solved nor as an illness to be 'treated', but first and foremost as a beloved son and lovely soul and she is rightly wary of suggestions that he be subjected to the barbaric horrors of shock treatment, or electro-convulsive 'therapy'. She reminds us, too, that motherhood is a sacrifice, not in a negative way but as the heart's offering up of something—or someone—treasured as sacred. Above all, Brigid and her family's shared voyage of discovery reminds us that we are all wounded by life and that with lightness and depth of being, acceptance and love, we can help one another limp and dance through it.

For those of you facing life with a loved one in a similar kind of non-violent acute crisis, I encourage you—if you have the inner and outer moral support you need—to take heart, be brave and follow where the journey guides you. As this story brings home, at worst you may end up emotionally drained, bewildered, frustrated and dismayed, for such is often the price of empathy and 'com-passion' (literally the ability to 'suffer with'). At best you will attain wisdom, patience, an ability to 'go with the flow' (Tao), deeper love and self-awareness, as well as an understanding and appreciation of the intricate dynamics and self-creativity of the psyche.

Finally, I hope you will be as enriched and educated by this rare offering as I have been. I feel honoured to be invited to endorse this special book and I do so unreservedly and with all my heart.

Maureen B. Roberts, PhD
Soul-centred Psychiatric & Shamanic Therapist
www.psychiatrywithsoul.com
www.jungcircle.com

Life with Mikey

I cried and cried. I couldn't stop; the tears kept coming. The nurses were concerned, at times annoyed. The obstetrician said I was allowed to cry—there was a lot to be sad about. My partner Simon was gone. He'd moved out with his toddler, Chloe, in the middle of the night and went back to Chloe's mum. "Potts and Gallagher: pig farmers" had been our dream of having a property in the Tasmanian mountains—a hobby farm and six children. Winter people, we loved crackling fires, heavy coats, warm fluffy gloves and rain. From the first moment I met Simon I knew that all my Christmases had come at once. My children Tara, Sam, Amelia-Jane and Timmy adored Simon and his golden-haired baby girl. I believed he would bring Chloe back to me at the last minute. Together with our newborn baby we would sail to Tasmania to begin our new life as a family. My home in Adelaide was sold, the boat tickets booked. I decided to stick to our plan, certain that he would, too.

A Perfect Baby

"You have a strapping young lad," the voice whispered near my ear. On November 10th 1986 Michael was delivered prematurely by Caesarean section under a general anaesthetic. It had been a difficult pregnancy. I developed gestational diabetes and was inconsolably tearful about the many changes occurring in my life. The obstetrician suggested I see a psychologist, which I did. I couldn't stop crying in the weeks following the delivery. My long curly hair fell out in clumps; blood tests showed I was depleted of vitamin B and iron and I seemed incapable of coping with the excruciating pain of a broken heart and shattered dreams.

Michael was a well-formed baby weighing nine pounds, classically beautiful, with translucent skin and big, dark eyes. He was born without eyebrows and eyelashes, both of which grew within a month. As a newborn, Michael did not cry or fuss. He melted into my arms during feeds and was limp to hold. I was puzzled about my sleepy, rag doll baby, but the hospital paediatrician said he was perfect and not to worry, adding with a grin that I'd gotten it right this time.

Brigid's perfect baby

Michael was my heart's joy; I felt blessed to have such an easy baby and was comforted by the diagnosis of "perfect". Michael continued to be floppy and never cried to be picked up, although he showed no resistance when I did. He stiffened rigidly when I lowered his little body into the bath water. I had never known a baby to be so distressed. It was like trying to bathe a wooden scarecrow and because it was upsetting for both of us, I chose to sponge bathe him instead.

In the days following Michael's birth the paediatrician noted an anal fissure, assuring me it would heal. However, over the next three years the fissure proved resistant to treatment. A constant smelly pus discharged and abscesses formed. Several doctors looked at it and recommended I keep the area clean. As well, Michael screamed from what seemed to be lower back pain. He would writhe and arch his back. The doctor said there was nothing wrong and noted the coincidence of the full moon each time Michael was in pain.

Michael was unusually placid and unresponsive to the everyday hustle and bustle of a busy family of six. In one sense, he could have been described as too good. I was enchanted with my baby boy; I adored everything about him and was deeply content to sit for hours cuddling him. He seemed undisturbed by strangers holding him and was always limp and passive when picked up, making him easy to cuddle. People were attracted to him even though he did nothing remotely interesting. He didn't smile or coo, yet people seemed fascinated with him, commenting on what an exquisitely lovely baby he was. He was indeed beautiful; symmetrical in his facial features, pretty to look at. Michael was my perfect baby.

Gypsy Blessing & Dream House

I still wonder about the old Gypsy woman who predicted Michael's birth. Appearing out of nowhere, she approached me in a crowded bakery in the city one lunchtime. Touching my belly, she told me that in fourteen days I would give birth to a baby boy. I told her that the baby wasn't due for another four or five weeks, but she remained firm. I dismissed the Gypsy's chatter even when fourteen days later, I gave birth to a baby boy. Later in the bakery, when Michael was three weeks old—his original due date—I did not notice the Gypsy until she stood before me, reached out and took my baby in her arms, then made a sign on his forehead with her thumb while she muttered something. She said it was a blessing, though I did not hear the words. Handing him back to me, she said she knew he would come and that he was going to be a great healer in the world.

Weeks passed; Christmas was over. Simon did not respond to the letters I sent along with the photographs of our little son Michael. The children and I drove seven hundred kilometres to Port Melbourne and boarded the ship to Tasmania. None of us had ever sailed before. It was exciting and the children played and ran all over the boat while I cuddled Michael in the cabin. He had a mild fever and seemed unwell and very sleepy.

It was a relief to be on land the next morning. I went to a medical clinic because Michael was trembling and vomiting. The doctor said the baby was seasick. Arriving on the island with four children, an eight week old baby, and only a tent to live in was an adventure full of unforeseeable challenges. We camped under pine trees, quite close to the beach. It was lovely, except that the tent leaked, the weather was freezing and it rained every day, even though it was summer. I abandoned the camping holiday and rented a house for a few weeks. A private advertisement in a local paper led me to a farm house for sale in a rural area I would not have considered, had I not been so exhausted.

I remembered from as far back as high school a clear vision of a long house with many rooms, in which ceiling to floor windows gave the impression that the house was made of glass. On the soft, mossy lawn stood a blue spruce tree. Red roses cascaded from trellises and boughs and flowers of a myriad shapes and forms filled the air with a heady scent. The rooms overflowed with children's laughter, books, toys, dolls, big furry teddies and little metal cars. This was my recurring dream, the place I went to while I slept.

The children and I bought a map and enjoyed the drive to the property, which had only been on the market for a few days. On the bank of a large river, by a bridge, was the house I dreamed of repeatedly, along with the red roses, the blue spruce tree and a vast expanse of windows. The owner wanted to show me inside. I told her I already knew what it was like. I did go in, overwhelmed with emotion. It was literally the house of my dreams. I bought it immediately and the children and I named it "Brambly Hedgerow". I wandered down to the bridge and let my gaze drift upstream, believing in that moment that I could never be unhappy again.

Brigid and baby Michael at Brambly Hedgerow

Rainbow Changes

During Michael's first year, I met various people who didn't like children yet who expressed a genuine desire to hold him. Somehow, they seemed different after the cuddle. It was as if Michael's presence imparted peace and exuded a deep love. This phase ended abruptly when he was around eighteen months old, when Michael could not be touched by strangers or even visiting friends. He would shy away, or cry out as if in terror. I was alarmed at and confused by the change in my placid baby.

After breastfeeding for eighteen months, I weaned Michael very slowly. He could smell a cup of tea from a room away and insisted on having a few drops of tea in his bottle of milk. This was the onset of bewildering eating habits and likes. For weeks he would only eat Weet-Bix with milk and honey and then suddenly would eat only broccoli and pumpkin. Michael ate using his thumb and forefinger as pincers and in this way touched and picked up everything. It was impossible for him to hold a spoon or fork so he was spoon-fed for years. It was very difficult getting him to eat anything at all. I kept a bowl of hundreds and thousands on the table and sprinkled them on whatever I offered him to eat. It worked well most of the time, since the tiny, rainbow-coloured freckles fascinated him. Friends criticised, concerned I was being manipulated by a toddler. Perhaps I was, but it didn't feel like that; it felt more like sharing a special discovery, or speaking a language without words.

Michael never babbled, although he sometimes gurgled if we were alone. He never said "mum" or "bub". His first word was "meelya". He was trying to say his sister Amelia's name. As a toddler he stuttered so badly that it could take days to discover what he was trying to say. It was exhausting for everyone and often Michael would give up. He slept beside me in a big, rickety farm bed and woke several times a night. I'd put the kettle on to make cups of sweet, milky tea and we'd tuck into a tray of bread and butter and biscuits. During our midnight feasts I read aloud, sometimes asking questions, sometimes answering them. I'm not sure when I stopped noticing that I was the only one speaking.

Michael wasn't interested in playing games such as touching my nose, then his nose, or pointing to my eyes then his, or putting his fingers in my mouth while I was talking. Concerned that as the youngest of five children he would be overindulged, I started Michael at a daycare centre in town for half a day each week. The supervisor told me that Michael sat in the shade at the far end of the building and could not be encouraged to do any activity. He was frantic and screamed when I left him and after discussing the situation, I chose not to take him again. This was the start of Michael's clinging desperation to always be with me.

Cocoon & Monsters

The children had sheepskins to lie on. Michael liked to press a small piece cut from one corner against his nose and breathe through the fluff. We called it "wormie", and everywhere Michael went wormie went, too. The simple piece of soft fur was so comforting that Michael would close his eyes, no matter where we were. One day on our way through town, wormie blew out of the car window and Michael bellowed such an ear-piercing scream that I nearly drove off the road. When he was eight, he wandered over to a pile of soft, fluffy floormats in a department store and fell asleep standing up. He often made a tiny ball from fluff he picked from his clothes, balanced the fluff on his nostrils and snorted it into the air.

Michael was an unusual child who seemed to flow through daily events like a trickle of water finding its way along a dry, rocky creek bed after the first rain following a drought. He didn't so much avoid things; he simply did not seem to have a need to interact with them. He was a pale, sickly, gentle toddler. He sat and could stare for hours at one thing. He liked to spin my wedding ring on his thumb, staring at it as though mesmerised.

While I was at work for a few hours each week, he would contentedly sit near me on a fluffy rug in a cardboard box. He never attempted to get out and never grizzled. He had a blue button tied to a piece of string and liked twirling it. From the age of two, he was preoccupied with drawing caterpillars on his easel blackboard. Visitors to our home were silently coerced into drawing butterflies for Michael, but he drew only caterpillars. A caterpillar spins itself into a cocoon, where a mysterious transformation takes place and later a butterfly emerges and flies away.

A quiet, seemingly invisible child, independent and happiest when left to himself, Michael displayed neither joyful excitement nor disappointment. He did not show emotion, apart from terror and a morbid fear of dying. Constantly troubled by ear infections, allergies, colds, asthma and stomach aches, he woke many times throughout the night. At two years old he began to suffer waking night terrors. The doctor said not to worry. The night terrors became nightmares. Michael was convinced the monsters in his dreams were real and in his room. While in the car at the supermarket carpark, without warning or apparent reason, he became agitated and frightened. Almost impossible to comfort, he collapsed in my arms, limp and pale. When he was older, he told me that he had seen a big bloodshot eye that day in the carpark. As the years passed, whenever he saw the eye something terrible happened.

Michael has always heard and seen people, monsters and disturbing beings that others cannot perceive. This does not mean he is psychic, though some would argue that he is, given that he has predicted events in our family which did happen. Michael is not particularly creative, or imaginative; he never pretends and has never invented games to play. Perhaps his monsters may in some sense be real.

Bubbles

Water Child Conductor

Our home was built on the bank of a large river and Michael, who was afraid of the water, liked sitting on a huge tree which had fallen across. An old crayfish lived underneath in a burrow. The Tasmanian freshwater crayfish is the largest freshwater invertebrate in the world, listed as endangered and only found in Tasmanian rivers flowing north into the Bass Strait. We could access the river during the short summer when the water was shallow, exposing the giant log. The crayfish was shy and secretive but if we sat quietly she emerged and we watched her in the crystal clear water scratching about in the pebbles and sand. In the late afternoon, mountain trout jumped out of the water to catch little insects. Michael enjoyed watching the fish and yet his overwhelming fear of water continued. When he was three, a family outing to the beach ended when he clung to the car door screaming in terror and could not be comforted. He could not look at the ocean. I sighed deeply, feeling sad and lonely. It was a glorious day, with a gentle sea breeze, rock pools glistening in the sunshine, buckets, spades and a big basket of picnic lunch. Perhaps next time . . .

I bought a small paddling pool and sometimes Michael could be coaxed to sit in it. I filled the pool with warm bubble bath so that he wouldn't see the water and in this way he was bathed. I had never known a child so terrified of getting wet. Having toilet trained four children, I did not expect problems with Michael, but he was terrified of using a potty and even more hysterical about seeing his pee squirt out.

Michael was not an active child, although he did some unusual things. While I stood by the window during a phone conversation, my attention was taken by the herd of eighty cows in the paddock beside the house. The cows cantered along the fence line to the far end of the paddock, then turned and cantered back past the house. I ended my call abruptly and ran outside to find Michael in his T-shirt and nappy, completely surrounded by cows. He had crawled through a gap in the fence. This was the first of his many fearless encounters with potential danger. I was astonished. It looked like he was conducting the wind, but it wasn't the wind—it was a mass of huge animals.

As a young child, Michael listened to the same record repeatedly—the Hans Anderson fairytale "The Emperor's New Clothes." I bought an old record player for him to use in his room because the continual repetition was frazzling. He had two videos that he watched, then rewound and watched again and again. He memorised parts of the dialogue and could sometimes recite them on command. It was cute and I enjoyed the sound of his voice.

House on Fire

Ice formed on the inside of the windows; the rain pelted relentlessly on the roof. With Michael cradled in my arms, I shivered and snuggled further down under the blankets. In June 1990 our family home caught ablaze in the middle of the night. My teenage children were away with friends. Timmy, Michael's older brother, was still on an extended holiday with my parents in Adelaide, following our visit over Christmas. I asked my mother to let him stay, since I was struggling to cope with the violence and weirdness of his temporal lobe epilepsy and undiagnosed autistic behaviour. Only Amelia-Jane and Michael were home with me on the night of the fire. I woke up wheezing as flames flicked through my bedroom door. I threw the children into the car as the house exploded.

The next morning, standing in the drizzling rain, staring at the smouldering rubble that only hours ago was our lovely home, I wondered what had happened to my life. A little hand grasped my wrist; Michael wanted his spoon. He suffered from smoke inhalation and asthma, but seemed alright following a medical check-up at the hospital, so we flew to Adelaide to stay with my parents. Michael had an acute asthma attack in the middle of the first night. He was taken by ambulance to the nearest hospital for oxygen and admitted to the infectious diseases ward for a week. I stayed with him. Confused about his isolation, I vaguely remember being told that he was suspected of having rotavirus, the most common cause of severe fever and diarrhoea in young children.

My two older children became as chaff on the wind and drifted about, staying with friends and spending money fearlessly. Amelia-Jane boarded with a farming family back in Tasmania and continued her regular school routine. Timmy remained settled at the primary school near my parents' home in Adelaide. Michael was old enough to begin kindergarten, but when I enquired about enrolment I was told it wasn't possible because of council policy restrictions about residency. An Aboriginal childcare centre was willing to have him attend and I gratefully accepted their offer.

The Aboriginal children were loving and sharing. It seemed they could do no wrong; there was no squabbling, or need for adult intervention. The staff were gentle and humbly accepted each child as an individual. Michael did not speak or join in, neither did he cry, or sit in a corner. He willingly went each morning, except Fridays when the group went on planned bus trips and ate a picnic lunch. Michael firmly resisted and nothing could get him on that bus.

Boy in a Box

Exactly one year after the fire we moved into our newly built home. Michael had his own room but refused to sleep in a bed. He wanted to sleep in a cardboard box. I bought two refrigerator boxes and joined them together. A flap from one into the other was only big enough for a small child to squeeze through and Michael would disappear into his cardboard womb with his sheepskin and battery operated lantern. I asked him why he needed to sleep in a box and he replied, "My needs a roof on my bed because something goes clunk on my head and lights get in my eyes." It was as if he were reconstructing his birth.

Michael went on to tell me why he was frightened of water and must not let it get on him. He accurately described the nurse at the small hospital where he was born, eerily detailing her face and uniform. He described the perspex crib on wheels that doubled as a bath. How could he know that? I was the only maternity patient that week and she and I had a petty argument about bathing Michael. I was wretched and miserable after the birth; the stitches hurt and my heart was broken; tears streamed down my cheeks even when I was sure I had no more left to cry. I phoned Simon's mum and told her that little Michael was born. I wondered why Simon hadn't come to see his son. I told the nursing sister I would bath my baby when I went home, but she insisted he be bathed and so she bathed him. Michael told me she let go of him and he sank under the water with his eyes wide open.

Michael feeding the seagulls (without looking at the water)

Michael was toilet-trained in time to start school, comforted in knowing that we were keeping his pee in the underground septic tank. During his first year at school, he wet his pants frequently and this distressed the staff. I packed a clean change of clothes every day. Michael was easily exhausted and was left asleep in a corner of the classroom each afternoon. On arriving home he would fall asleep before tea time. The school deemed a home visit necessary and a staff member spent one morning at our house. Michael went about his usual routines. The teacher said this was not the child she knew and asked me cheerily if I switched him at the school yard gate each day. Michael continued his silence and I was told that nobody at school ever heard him speak. Timmy, who was at the same school, was noted to be autistic by a special education teacher. He was prone to several forms of seizure, temporal lobe epilepsy being the most dangerous because of the associated violence. I was nervous that Timmy would injure another child. He was strikingly handsome but a real handful, needing much patience and understanding.

The year during which our home was rebuilt left our family fragmented. Having experienced freedom and notoriety, the teenagers refused to settle, choosing to create turmoil and distress. Every day was fraught with loud noise, arguing and excessive physical, emotional and verbal abuse. They left home together only months after moving into our new house. I worried that Michael would be upset about the changes in our family structure but he seemed the same, as though nothing had happened. I wished I could be like him.

Games and Hobbies

Michael didn't play with toys. For his sixth birthday he wanted a dozen eggs. I invited classmates to a party. Michael insisted he didn't know the boys, even though they were in his class. The boys ran about squealing and chasing each other while Michael sat in his cubby-house clutching his birthday eggs. While he was using the toilet, a few boys took the eggs and smashed them. The mothers were embarrassed and with a sense of urgency, we replaced the broken eggs with fresh ones from the kitchen. Michael realised the eggs were not the same. He was heartbroken and cried and cried.

Michael had a wooden box of small metal cars which he played with in his room. He would take the first car, line it up with the box then smash a chosen car into it. He did this to each car in turn, then repeated the process. He always put the cars neatly back in the box when he had finished.

From an early age, Michael was fascinated with alchemy and mixed potions with exactness of ingredients, order and method at the same time each day. He had a straw-bale cubby specially designed for brewing his mixtures in. Ingredients included grasses he gathered and grocery items such as sugar, salt, flour and eggs. It was all real to him.

Cooking with dough

Fascinated with dinosaurs, sharks and wizards, Michael turned his room into a museum of rocks, glass bottles, bones and a variety of shark and animal teeth. He had his appendix removed when he was four and kept the stitches in a bottle, along with a fingernail that fell off his crushed finger and all his baby milk teeth. On his tenth birthday he asked for rocks and a weekend rock-hounding expedition to the Tasman Peninsula filled yet another shoe box with fossils and crystals.

At the age of five, Michael abruptly stopped drawing white chalk caterpillars on his blackboard. Notebooks were filled with complicated pencil drawings from a bird's eye view; they resembled floor or engineering plans, highly detailed within a neat lined frame. The graphics conveyed black and white factual information rather than artistic expression. He kept his notebooks and pencils in old tins inside a carved wooden box with a brass latch and key.

When Michael was seven, we were walking along the beach and he asked me how far I could count before I had to swallow my spit. I chuckled and squeezed his little hand, wondering how he thought of such things. He counted unusual items—stairs, footsteps between shops—anything and everything. In restaurants Michael sat in his fluffy kangaroo sleeping bag on the floor beside me, drawing in his notebook. Everyone adored him but nobody dared touch him. He had a sort of aura surrounding him, an invisible sign that warned, "Look, but don't touch." He did acknowledge Natasha, the manager at our favourite bistro. One evening while Natasha and I chatted,

Michael asked her for a cup of milky tea. Hours later we noticed how swollen his tummy was; he had asked for and drunk seven cups of tea. From that night on, we called it the "cup of tea splurge."

It was easy to become absorbed in Michael's repetition and not realise that an apparent purpose lurked behind it. Michael drank seven cups of tea and was seven years old. While this may seem absurd, it is typical of the kind of autistic numerical association Michael used every day.

Black and White and Red

I liked the small, crowded café in Burnie; it was intimate, cosy and friendly. I often bumped into rural neighbours, or friends from the jazz club. There was always opportunity to make a new acquaintance, too. Michael spent the time stepping along the diagonal lines of black and white tiles. As he got older he counted the tiles. We visited the café for many happy years before it sold. The walls were painted bright pink and the furniture repositioned so that Michael couldn't walk along the straight line of tiles. The new staff didn't like him tiptoeing about and refused to serve cold milk because it wasn't on the menu.

Michael went through a stage where he liked to eat from a bowl on the floor, although he preferred to eat outside with the bowl nestled in the grass. It seemed to be connected with his fascination of dinosaurs and all food had tomato sauce splattered over it. I took Michael and my young cousins to the cinema to see *Jurassic Park*. My Uncle was surprised when he arrived home to find the boys kneeling on the floor eating chunks of roast meat swimming in tomato sauce. Michael didn't react to the outburst, but he never ate sauce again.

Michael's school experience was neither enjoyable nor nurturing. He had no interest in class activities or friendship with other children. I transferred him to a coastal town school, hoping he would be happier. We both enjoyed the sixteen kilometre drive each way but things became exceedingly worse. Michael had been ignored in the small rural school, but in town he was bullied and physically harmed by the other children. His school work was scribble and when I pressed him for a reason, he said that he couldn't let anyone know anything about him. When Michael did speak he stuttered badly and was unable to form certain sounds. Joining "f" and "th" together, for example, changed the word "death" into "deafth"; replacing the letter "k" with "qu", turned the word "pumpkin" into "pumpquin." He was teased at school for his speech and idiosyncratic use of language. Although Michael did not complain about being teased, he became silent again.

Both of us were frequently in trouble. I was given the notary title of "problem parent of the year," while Michael was named a "sook." I watched Michael stand dazed and rigid in class while the teacher continued to yell. Seemingly incapable of understanding instruction, he took everything literally and became overly anxious when forced to participate in activities. Without my knowing, Michael was sent to a remedial class for most of each day. I would never have known if one of the mums hadn't mentioned it in passing. Michael whispered in my ear every day after school, "I'm not safe—I don't feel looked after." The teacher was intimidating, the pressure to conform mind-numbing.

Strange Waters

I had neglected my health over the years. I collapsed and was admitted to hospital for a hysterectomy. A family friend offered to care for Michael but sent Amelia-Jane and Timmy to their estranged father in Adelaide. My parents, my older children and extended family abandoned us at this time. I never understood why. The four older children, now with their Egyptian father, became increasingly alienated from me; the cultural differences between us seemed to create a huge gulf of silence. Michael didn't appear to miss his brothers and sisters at all.

Fully recovered from the surgery, I sold our riverbank home and bought a beach cottage on a cliff overlooking Bass Strait. Michael spent endless hours sitting among the huge rocks above the sea. Fishermen returned in their boats with empty nets but young Michael was catching fish from the rocks faster than he could haul them in. Only seven years old, he caught a large salmon.

Michael and his big catch

Neighbours and friends were completely astonished that Michael had caught the fish on his own. A fisherman suggested that the fish had bashed against a rock—making it easier to reel in—but even so it was a big catch. Primary Industries in Hobart identified several peculiar fish Michael caught—species never before seen in southern Australian waters.

Michael row your boat onshore

Living by the beach was delightful and everyday life took on a comfortable routine. The neighbours were friendly, the cafes welcoming and there was enough money for weekend trips away. I immersed myself in the community and started a blues-rock get-together at the hotel every Friday night. The locals enthusiastically encouraged me to open a jazz club with a group of musicians.

Being elected president of the school's Parent Group, I felt more accepted by the staff; however, it wasn't long before I was confronted about Michael's pattern of non-attendance. He was simply unable to endure the full five day week and spent every Friday at home, asleep. He couldn't cope with the classroom commotion and whimpered in response to a noise in the back of his head. He cried and said it was like a radio he couldn't turn off.

A group of friendly mums invited me to join them at a private indoor heated pool every day after school. The children were younger than Michael with the exception of two teenage girls. As usual Michael wouldn't get into the water. He stood shivering on the cold tiles watching the teenagers diving and swimming, then quite unexpectedly trotted past me to the far end of the pool and dived in. It was deep and a lot of splashing and gasping resulted, but in just a few days Michael swam underwater like a little fish. I was confident that he could impress the teachers with his swimming ability, but the school swimming instructor at the public pool refused permission for Michael to wear his nose plug. The instructor shouted to each child in turn to dunk their face under the water. Michael froze and wouldn't put his head down. He was left in the shallow with a small plastic bucket to tip water over his head until he stopped being afraid. A mother urged me to get him out of the pool; trembling and pale, he passed out in my arms. Michael did not swim in a pool again until he was fourteen and began private sessions with a woman who had coached some of Australia's Commonwealth Games swimming team. Michael showed great potential during the first few weeks, then became increasingly reluctant to continue.

The young man and the sea

Classical music is one of my great pleasures. Michael liked to curl up at my feet while I played the piano. When he was snuggled with a pillow on the floor and his back pressed against the wooden front panel, the banging above him created a resonating chamber. The older children each played a musical instument. Michael learned the violin, did very well and showed great sensitivity. A particularly haunting tune disturbed him; each time he played it, he would run outside to vomit. The amazed tutor asked if Michael knew the history of the piece. Cromwell's invasion of Ireland in 1650 AD was a brutally bloodthirsty time in Irish history and this tune was played by the fife and drum band as the English soldiers marched their Irish captives to the gallows.

Michael playing his violin

At parent-teacher interview I mentioned our love of music and that Michael was learning the violin. The lessons were frowned upon and his ability to write strings of programming code in DOS, bluntly disbelieved. The meeting was a crippling revelation.

Magic Food for Thought

School presented problems for Michael at lunch time. From the age of seven, he refused to eat or drink anything outside of our home. He believed someone was going to poison him. I could not find anything to entice him, until one day he wanted to eat some of his dog's biscuits. I didn't mind him chewing them at home, but I feared the staff would misunderstand the desperation I felt in trying to get Michael to eat.

Michael liked to whiz and whirl himself into a dizzy faint. I felt dizzy just watching him. He loved to walk between Amelia-Jane and me; holding hands we'd swing him up into the air with every step we took. Michael wore the toes of his leather boots completely away every three weeks by kneeling on the asphalt at school and spinning himself.

Invented routines and rituals helped Michael cope with school. I placed a silk square on the floor near the front door. Michael put personal power objects on each corner of the square and would stand in the centre, while I sprinkled silver and gold glitter onto him from above. He said that the glitter had the magical power to keep him safe at school. The ritual was successful, but one morning, when a woman came to pick up documents I had written for her, she trampled over the silk and the sacred space was destroyed.

School Daze and Happy Days

Frantic about attending school, Michael begged me in terror not to leave him. He suffered acute attacks of asthma and was always itchy. He insisted on wearing a woollen beanie pulled down over his eyebrows. The teachers tried to pull it off but Michael held it on with his fists. He was pushed roughly about in class and suffered three broken fingers in one year. He seemed completely confused in the classroom and just stood, or sat wide-eyed and pale. It was as if he were alone in a storm.

He had always been clingy and silent when out of the house—a well-behaved though very serious little boy. When visiting, he would slide into a house as if glued to me, then hide behind the nearest curtain and stand there till it was time to leave. Mothers adored him but kids thought him weird. The taunts and teasing from classmates became unbearable. I didn't notice that I had stopped visiting people who had children.

Michael petting a wild wallaby in a Tasmanian forest.

Michael was inconsolably unhappy at school and no longer able to turn a blind eye to it, I investigated alternatives. A private Christian college offered an external, distance education program. With the initial interview and academic examination completed, Michael was enrolled. Colourful workbooks emphasised Christian ideals, goal-setting and flexibility, teaching children to take responsibility for their own learning. Michael grew and put on weight; people commented on how well he looked. He slotted the school assignments into his fishing schedule while we travelled around Tasmania and visited places of historical interest on mainland Australia.

Those years were very happy for us both. A perfectionist in everything, Michael was given the only Diligence Award the college ever presented and scored high marks for academic achievement. No longer seeking guidance from my family, friends and doctor, I was convinced I had done what was right for Michael and me. Having completed his high school studies, Michael wanted to continue computer programming at a tertiary level but at fourteen was too young to attend class, so he enrolled with the flexible delivery option. On the first night he powered through a third of the thick book. I smiled and said, "Michael, it's a six month course—not three days!"

Boy in a Bubble

As a child, Michael ignored being spoken to; he would turn his back on the person speaking to him. As a teenager he would look anywhere but at a person's face. He never looked at himself in a mirror, did not recognise himself in photographs and never made eye contact with anyone, including me. Many people have never heard him speak. He existed in his own world, unconcerned by the comings and goings of people and events around him, but affected by changes in his own physical world. For him, new phenomena may be added, but nothing can be removed, or replaced. His beliefs are rules etched in stone and cannot be altered or compromised. Michael doesn't understand feelings. He shows no empathy, laughing at the saddest and most tragic events.

Michael's reaction to having fingernails, toenails and hair cut seemed equal to the agony of having a limb amputated without anaesthetic. He preferred his hair long and parted in the middle. He became so anxious at the hairdresser's he would vomit and once even blacked out during a haircut.

Michael's clothing was simple and although that should make life easy, it didn't. From the age of seven, all clothes—including his underwear—had to be blue. By the time he was ten, all his clothing had to be black. He had three identical outfits. Every day he wore a clean set of clothes, but children teased him about never changing his style of clothing. I bought double of everything so that he never noticed the change from old to new. Michael would not wear trousers with a zip or buttons. All clothing was soft, loose and of a smooth, consistent texture. For him, clothing cannot display brand names. There cannot be a stripe, pattern, or additional stitching. Cuffs, necklines and bands must be loose, or nonexistent.

Home schooling was perfect for Michael. He enjoyed the colourful work books, became more passionate about fishing and grew tall and strong.

"Look at the Barracuda I caught!"

A few boys from the local school hung out at our beach cottage every weekend and during the holidays. Our garden shed was stuffed full of fishing gear, snorkels, boogie boards, bikes and discarded clothing. The shed was a hub of laughter and stench, where bait buckets overflowed with quivering clumps of maggots and rotting fish heads.

Fresh caught Mullet

The lads followed Michael into the sea as he leapt from rock to rock, never slipping or missing his footing. Holding his rod and bait bucket above his head, he waded across the reef, waves lapping at his throat. After a long day fishing, they cooked their catch over a camp fire and the delicious smell of buttery calamari, garfish, flathead and leatherjackets wafted on the sea breeze.

Man's two best friends—barbeque and dog

Michael had conquered his fear of the sea and had become one with it, spending hours each day snorkelling the reef. A graceful stingray and her pup lived in a shallow, sandy bay protected from the open ocean by steep outcrops of volcanic rock. Each day she was there and Michael hand-fed her crabs and tiny fish. Diving in, he swam closely above her until she tired of the company and headed out to the deep sea. The men who knew of her were obsessed with catching and killing the creature and one sad day they shouted their triumph.

Amelia-Jane finished her studies in Adelaide and moved in with us; she was great fun to live with and a fantastic cook. They were happy years living by the beach. When Michael was sixteen, he began to feel lonely and desperately wanted his friendships to remain intact. However, the boys who used our shed as a fishing base grew older and found new interests, which included girls and sports. They came less often, then not at all, and Michael was alone again.

Amelia-Jane had purchased a small ramshackle farm property in the mountains, which turned out to be a rather challenging project. Surrounded by forests inhabited by spotted-tail quolls, wombats and of course possums and wallabies, it was a wilderness wonderland. The Tasmanian Wedge-Tailed Eagle is almost black in colour and we were thrilled to watch the magnificent birds circle the tree tops. Tasmanian Devils were breeding under the house and although the pups were cutely amusing, the noise and smell was oppressive and we were glad when they moved out. A large tiger snake had taken up residence in the roof but it, too, left, disturbed by our renovations. We treated the property as a job, spending eight hours each day demolishing, rebuilding and clearing the sheds of junk. I accepted an unexpectedly generous offer from a tourist to buy the beach cottage in November 2003 and we all moved to the mountains to live on Amelia-Jane's hobby farm.

Emergency Surgery

The day following our move, Michael collapsed in a pool of blood and pus, and used an entire roll of toilet paper trying to soak up the mess. Terrified he was dying, he confessed he'd hidden this painful infection for the past few years. While I waited for the doctor's surgery to return my call for an appointment time, we sprawled on the grass in the sunshine, stunned and silent. On several occasions I had spoken to our family doctor about a smelly yellow discharge on Michael's underwear. Stupidly, I was told that it was sweat and that the smell was bothering me because I wasn't used to living with a man. Amelia-Jane drove us to the clinic where the doctor examined Michael's bleeding wound, then referred him to a surgeon for an urgent consultation.

The surgeon couldn't make a concise diagnosis because of the extent of the infection, referring Michael to a colon rectal specialist in Launceston, some 200kms away. The diagnosis was Pilonidal Sinus, though there was discussion regarding the possibility of Spina Bifida Occulta, a condition resulting from abnormal development of the spinal nerve roots and chord, causing a spinal deformity. The surgeon was appalled that the infection had continued since birth without any medical investigation. The small anal fissure and resistant abscesses had never healed completely and the infection had spread throughout Michael's body. X-rays showed his spine was twisted. I reflected on the numerous falls and crashes he suffered as a child. He was not quite four when he climbed the ladder of a very high slippery-dip. I didn't notice him follow Timmy. My foot on the first rung, my heart pounding, I looked up to see little Michael take his hands off the rails. "Hold on," I screamed. His body floated past me and landed crumpled on the grass. A doctor checked him for concussion; he appeared to be alright—not even a bruise. I wondered if the fall could have damaged his spine.

It was assumed that the infection had spread into the colon and so Michael's surgery was deemed urgent and more extensive than anticipated. I drove him home from hospital on Christmas Eve. It was a cruel hour and poor Michael groaned with every bump in the road. On Christmas morning the community nurses arrived to change the dressings and pack the wound. Michael's needs had not been clearly explained. We were all unprepared for what would be required each day. Michael had a huge hole the size of a man's fist between his anus and natal cleft. It was certainly nothing trivial.

The gaping wound needed to be packed with seaweed wadding. Every day, more than an hour before the nurses arrived, Michael lay soaking in a salt bath to soften the packing before it was removed. In hospital he had been given morphine. At home we used Endone and Ibuprofen. Michael could barely walk and needed Amelia and me for support. Sitting was impossible and he had to stand to use the toilet. The infection spread and eight weeks later a second surgery was necessary. Michael became pale and increasingly withdrawn. The nurses noticed and suggested I speak to our family doctor about possible depression. He was treated repeatedly for ear infections and bronchitis. The wound was exceedingly slow to heal. A third surgery was discussed, but Michael was considered too unwell. The surgeon showed me how he wanted the wound packed and dismissed the community nurses. I felt very alone; the nurses had been my lifeline. I felt beaten physically—the smell of the saturated seaweed wads was nauseating. Causing my boy pain during the daily nursing procedure tore at my heart and tears rolled down my face. Months passed and although the wound closed, the skin was fragile and split open repeatedly.

Michael continued his studies from bed on a laptop. Disregarding constant pain and the side-effects of prescription medications, he persevered and completed Certificate IV in Information Technology (Programming), compulsively deleting and rewriting his code in his striving for perfection. Michael then enrolled in the Online Programming Diploma from the Launceston TAFE campus and also began university mathematics.

Moving On

In March 2004 I bought Michael a classic 1970 Holden Kingswood Ute for $3,250. The car remained parked in the shed until he was well enough to sit comfortably. Amelia-Jane taught him to drive and he loved it. He drove her into town on errands, to the beach and anywhere she cared to go, but he wouldn't get out of the car.

Michael and Amelia-Jane attended the Tasmanian University Summer School physics bridging course, which included overnight stays in Hobart. Michael did all the driving and enjoyed the busy city traffic. I was amazed at the change in his disposition, though he did insist on taking packed food and a plastic bowl and teaspoon. He found the course useful for his computer programming, but did not actively participate, or speak aloud.

Our family Christmas tradition is to chop down and decorate a pine tree on the 1st day of December. In the past Michael had chosen the tree months before. December began but Michael wasn't interested in finding a Christmas tree, discussing presents, or choosing a festive food menu. He is very traditional and I felt baffled by his lack of interest. Weeks before Christmas, he received a large box of organic chilli powders which we'd ordered online from England. He prepared his own gourmet meal-sized snacks, which were hot enough to burn the skin off a rhinoceros. Michael offered to make our evening supper and cups of tea, which was pleasant but had never happened before.

On Christmas Eve morning, Michael walked out of his room announcing he had just submitted an online application for a job position. I didn't see that coming. "I'm moving to Launceston to train and work as a security guard," he said. I was stunned. On Christmas Day he refused to eat with us, making himself more hot spicy snacks instead. I was dismayed. This was not the Michael I knew at all. Over the summer he stopped doing things he had always enjoyed. Walking his dog became a drudgery. He refused to go to the beach and couldn't be jollied out of increasingly sullen moods, becoming easily irritated and grumpy. I was deeply worried; never in his life had he displayed either mood or emotion.

Listless and apathetic, he drifted in and out of sleep and when he wasn't asleep was doing something alarming and completely out of character. He insisted on chain-sawing and splitting wood. Increasingly finicky about household chores, he took over washing up; the dishes were rinsed, washed and rinsed again. The clothesline pegs were arranged in sets of type and colour. In the pantry, packets, boxes and tins were arranged in straight rows, labels facing front. There was a place for everything and everything was in its place.

Dramatic Changes

In early February, Michael passed his driving test and was able to drive his car alone. He liked the Kingswood but became obsessed with owning the latest Holden Crewman Ute, which sold for $50,000 and had leather seats, chrome roll bars and wheel mags, a state-of-the-art GPS navigational system, DVD player, fancy stereo and volume controls on the steering wheel.

Michael persisted in shopping every few days, a forty minute drive each way to town. During this time, he took an astonishing interest in his appearance, fussing with his hair, shaving twice daily and dressing up to go to the supermarket. He bought and tried new shampoos, specialist hair styling and skin care products and applied for various jobs, including truck driver, mechanic, ATM machine installer, supermarket night fill, seaweed harvester, armed security guard, forklift driver, quarantine dog trainer and apple picker. He longed to go apple picking. He and Amelia-Jane applied, passed the medical check but were offered positions in a carrot factory seventy-five kilometres from our home. The long, winding drive and eleven hour shifts were gruelling. After four days, Michael collapsed, pale and ill.

Recovering from yet another chest and ear infection, he responded to a job advertisement for a psychiatric attendant at the hospital. He phoned the ward and made an appointment to discuss the job criteria; an hour later he drove to the hospital. Several hours passed; he returned, downloaded the application forms and sighed. We both had difficulty understanding the government jargon and Michael was clearly unqualified for the job.

A drastic change occurred in Michael around his eighteenth birthday. I hoped he was coming out of himself now that his wound was healed. I found him alarmingly restless and animated, refusing to discharge what seemed an excessive amount of energy. He was highly charged with static electricity, getting shocks off supermarket shelves, trolleys, even tins of food. I didn't want to touch him—even our finger tips touching caused a static crackling sound and sharp pain.

Michael announced that he still wanted to train as an armed security guard and enrolled in an intensive training program in Melbourne, which guaranteed work at the 2006 Commonwealth Games. Amelia-Jane agreed to train with him; I was reluctant to go along with what felt like a bizarre demand and was adamant that he was not going alone. The accommodation and airfares were booked and paid for, yet Michael became more irritable and moody. I queried his grumpiness and in a deluge of tears, he told me he was only going to Melbourne because I wanted him to. I explained that this wasn't true and that I would be utterly relieved if he didn't go. His general mood was unsettled; he believed he had upset Amelia-Jane and me. Deeply remorseful and anxious, he repeatedly apologised for wasting a lot of money.

Although Michael has used idiosyncratic language since he was a child, his speech had never been garbled, or incoherent. Suddenly he was talking gibberish and at times gave up trying to speak, because he couldn't get the words right. I assumed he was teasing me, but he was truly frightened by the strange episodes. As examples, the following words "Yodaovtasloopiana," "hooden haffen," "copochoniella," "gunovtasloopy" and "imovtaslup" all meant "goodnight." He complained of bad headaches and of not being able to think straight. Michael and his Russian associate of the same age worked together on opposite sides of the world, creating a superior navigational flight simulator game. They met on the Internet and a friendship formed between our families as we communicated through an exchange of emails, parcels and letters between Australia and Moscow. I questioned Michael about his partnership commitment. He told me he was no longer interested in their project, nor had he done any work on his diploma. In fact he had deleted all the files.

Michael languished. By early June his appetite had noticeably diminished; he had lost eleven kilograms since Christmas. By July he had lost another four kilograms and was eating as little as possible. Fear clutched my heart. Was my precious son seriously ill again? The surgeries had been successful and the wound was completely healed, although the scar tissue was sensitive and delicate. There was reason to suspect that the infection might recur, but the specialist had given the all-clear for now. I wondered how Michael could lose more than 15% of his body weight in such a short time. The doctor brushed my worry aside, claiming it was part of the surgery aftermath. I didn't understand and no-one gave me a satisfactory explanation.

Amelia-Jane and I privately discussed our fears. We wondered who the new Michael was and more importantly, what had happened to the Michael we knew. It was bewildering. Perhaps to a stranger, Michael might have seemed to be simply growing up, since after almost a year he was feeling better.

Over the past year we had met several doctors at a new clinic, none of whom we were comfortable with. I asked around and a private doctor taking on new patients agreed to see us as a family. In July however, Michael secretly made an appointment with a clinic doctor we had decided was not right for us. Michael returned from the appointment with a prescription for antidepressant tablets, announcing he was leaving home for good. He packed a bag of clothes and told me he was going to Queensland with his Russian Wolfhound dog, Anatoli—named after the Russian mathematician.

It was late afternoon. Michael had no money and Anatoli was difficult to handle. Amelia and I questioned him about his plans, asking if he had somewhere to stay, as well as food, money and boat tickets. Michael gave unrealistic answers and became argumentative. Frantic, I exploded, wondering what his hurry was. Michael insisted he needed to leave. I burst into tears, fell into a chair and babbled apologies. Amelia-Jane quietly suggested we all talk about it in the morning. It was hard to realise what had just happened. Where had this huge, hot rush of hysteria come from? The house felt calm again. It was weird. I filled the kettle and turned around to see Michael turn white and physically collapse.

Amelia-Jane and I helped him into bed. The following afternoon Michael had still not emerged from his room. After no response to my knocking, I opened the door, gasped and caught my breath. Michael lay on the bed paralysed, unable to speak or move. At first glance he looked dead. I made an emergency appointment with our new family doctor, who started Michael on Luvox and referred him for immediate psychiatric evaluation.

I would like to be able to type "The End" but cannot. Michael's collapse was the beginning of a surreal and perilous journey and with fear as my angel and a large dose of courage, I write on . . .

Biting the Bullet

Dear Cynthia

Something wholly unexpected and dreadful has happened to Michael. I went into his room yesterday and he was paralysed and couldn't speak. His eyes were wide open, but he didn't blink. He just stared straight through me. It was difficult getting him into the car; he was stiff and floppy at the same time. Amelia-Jane drove us to the Medical Clinic where the doctor told me I should have called an ambulance. It seems Michael suffered a breakdown during the night. The doctor wanted him taken straight to the psychiatric ward of the hospital, but eventually agreed he could go home for the night. Michael was given some kind of medication and we left. We have an appointment at the psychiatric outpatient clinic this morning. Michael cannot speak and needs to be held up to walk. I will let you know what the psychiatrist thinks is wrong.

Brigid

Dear Cynthia

Our meeting with the psychiatrist was very upsetting. He says that Michael is severely depressed and needs to be admitted to the hospital for several weeks. When he said that Michael needs ECT I burst into tears. The psychiatrist asked how I knew what Electro-Convulsive Therapy is. I muttered something about One Flew Over the Cuckoo's Nest, *but he didn't know what I meant. He then went through every detail of the procedure and its side effects. I tasted vomit in the back of my throat. It's hard to understand what is happening and why.*

The small room had no window and only enough space for three chairs, but we squeezed four in. The psychiatrist sat with his legs wide apart. Amelia-Jane and I scrunched our legs together tightly and Michael jiggled uncontrollably. The psychiatrist was Indian and although he spoke English, there was a notable simplicity in the discussion. He asked me to write a twenty-five page history about Michael—I feel daunted about that. He faxed a prescription through to the Regional Hospital and we picked it up on the way home. I am confused about the tablets which have to be taken at various times, some with food. The writing on the bottles is very small and hard to read. The Risperidone is to be taken morning and night, the Fluvoxamine and Clonazapam at night. Michael has another appointment tomorrow, but for now he is snuggled in bed, fast asleep. Amelia-Jane is baking chocolate star-shaped biscuits and the divine smell is wafting through the house. I feel very shaken up and worried. I phoned mum, who says that Michael has a nasty virus. I don't think that's right. I don't know what could cause a healthy young man to become paralysed overnight. I can't believe it's happened. Michael has collapsed in every area of his being and is incapable of thought and action. I am scared Cynthia; very, very scared.

Fondly
Brigid

Dearest Cynthia

I Googled information about the tablets Michael is taking. I read that these are the usual medications for schizophrenia. I rang mum and she doesn't know how Michael could have gotten schizophrenia. I am wondering why he is on such medication. He woke up this morning clutching his chest, crying. He still does not speak and hasn't eaten or drunk anything, apart from a few mouthfuls of biscuit and sips of milk. It's been more than a week and I cannot see any improvement. Michael hasn't been to the toilet and just lies in bed drifting in and out of sleep. I gently stroke his hair and he just stares at the ceiling. What has happened to him? I don't know what to think.

With fondest regards
Brigid

Everything turned around overnight. Michael was talking. It was confusing, though, because many of his words didn't make sense. He said that the right half of his chest felt crushed in, as though a giant boulder had been dropped on it in the night. He was ice cold to touch, which seemed strange because the cottage was toasty warm. The tablets certainly seemed to be helping, although he had little or no appetite and was nauseous and dizzy. Looking at him lying in a king-size bed, eating from the tiniest bowl and a miniature spoon, I felt very Alice in Wonderland. He was obsessed about locking doors and his bedroom door had to be kept shut; I didn't know why, but I couldn't turn the knob most days. The more quietly I tried to open and close the door, the more rattling I seemed to make. When I gave it a good tug it banged. Michael really worried about doors. He'd never mentioned it before and I wondered about all the times I found myself locked both outside and in. He complained of being overly sensitive to sunlight and asked that the windows be covered with heavy drapes to shut out even the tiniest ray.

Michael lost more weight—I could feel his bones when I cuddled him. I bought a colourful tray, bowl, cup and plate to encourage him to eat. He wrote his "Eating Rules" in his journal for the psychiatrist:

Eating Rules.

My breakfast food ritual is as follows:

I must start the day with a bowl of Kellogg's Froot Loops in my plastic Winnie the Pooh bowl. I can't not have it in the Winnie the Pooh bowl. I couldn't eat it in another bowl. Then I can't eat anything else until I have some tuna and crisps. The tuna and crisps must be matching flavours, or it isn't okay to eat. If I try to eat anything between the Kellogg's Froot Loops and the tuna and crisps, I feel very freaked out for breaking my rules. The next meal must be cheese and double pickle sandwiches.

I can't eat any type of soup during the months of summer. I can't eat soup if there is less than 50% cloud coverage, or the temperature is 20 degrees Celsius. Soup cannot be eaten early in the day. It can't be eaten late in the day either. Between 12pm and before dark are acceptable hours for eating soup. I cannot eat salad during the months of autumn, winter and spring. I can't eat salad in summer if the temperature is below 20 degrees Celsius, or if there is more than 50% cloud coverage. Salad cannot be eaten early in the day; it must be eaten after 5pm. If I am going to eat flavoured wafer biscuits, I must have one of each flavour. If there isn't one of each flavour then I cannot eat any.

Although the Eating Rules looked limiting, I kept the pantry stocked with Mike's current menu choices. I adored him. Nothing was ever too much bother.

Dear Cynthia

We are all feeling anxious about today's appointment in the psychiatric clinic. Michael is absolutely terrified of the doctor and the cultural difference is huge. It is difficult getting the doctor to comprehend the times and dates of events. The language barrier is a deep concern, since some things Michael has said have been completely misinterpreted, which has created even more fear. I feel disempowered at present and this is causing me to be militantly protective of Michael. Thank you for acknowledging my feelings and fears. It is comforting.

Michael is already on 3mg of Risperidone daily. I think it is helping. It is not a drug he can suddenly stop taking, so we are a bit stuck for the present. Michael believes that the doctor is trying to kill him, so appointments are overwhelmingly stressful. He fears for his life.

Last night he had a dream about a black woman with no face. There was another younger black woman lying on a hospital bed with a scalpel stuck in her cheek. The cheek was bruised and bleeding. The woman with no face bent over the girl, pulled the scalpel out of the cheek and slit the girl's throat. Blood gushed out. The woman shut the door and she cannot pass through it. The door leads to the rest of the building, which is the only safe place. She bent over Michael and stabbed him in the heart. He woke up in horrible pain which lasted more than several minutes, then slowly eased. Michael says that this is not the first time the faceless woman has visited him. I wonder what this is about.

With fondest regards
Brigid

It was a long night. Michael heard a constant beeping sound close by and in the distance. When I couldn't find where it was coming from, he decided it mustn't be real. Yet if it was loud enough to keep him awake, wasn't that real? By 4am I gave up going back to bed, brewed a pot of tea and sat beside the wood stove with my knitting. Michael believed the Risperidone was unlocking his creativity. He showed me thirteen pencil drawings of the monsters he was frightened of as a young child. They are grotesque. Each drawing had an accompanying poem explaining the monster's mission and behaviour. There was a large drawing of the eye Michael saw when he was three. The pupil was white and horrible. "Dark Souls" is about the hooded men in our garden that Michael saw when he was three . . .

Dark Souls

The caped little men stand guard at my house
They let nothing past, not even a mouse.
Armed with a plastic shovel or some other toy,
Torture is what they inflict on this boy.
They bash and smash with all their might
This little boy gets filled with fright.
For these dark men are dressed in black
And their capes are worn a little slack.
The hoods they wear cover their faces
But I know they don't belong in this place.
One guards the sandpit out the back
Still as a statue is this man in black.
Still until I go near him
Then he beats me in light that is dim.
These men sure make their brutal mark
I know the souls of these men are dark.

I was so tired. I made my first contact with the Tasmanian Mental Illness Support Group in Hobart. I had an hour chat with several lovely people. I was told that when the carer resource guy got back from his holiday in August, he would make a time to visit us here at home. Meanwhile, I was welcome to phone the support service on the toll free number whenever I wished. Another branch of carer resources in Launceston was sending me a pile of information, too.

Michael had a review appointment with the psychiatrist the next morning. I was really nervous. I packed him a hospital-stay bag in the hope that if I packed it, he wouldn't need it. Michael had a weird episode on Monday night that frightened us. He said he heard me sobbing and the voice told him to hurt himself. He got up, boiled the kettle and poured the bubbling water over his hands. The poor darling boy then ran cold water over the skin and applied burn cream. He said he really wanted to slash his arms and stomach with the kitchen knives. He wanted to see gore. He wanted to see muscles slashed and gouged open—to see blood gushing out of his body. A cold, wet, trickling sensation ran down his arms and legs, making him want to cut deep into the flesh. In his journal he wrote, "I feel I have no future. I feel there is no place in this world for me."

He told me that last year—when he insisted on making cups of tea—he poured the boiling water over his hands. My heart sank. I was dismayed. I asked him about all the scars on his fingers and hands. Often he came home from the beach with bleeding hands when he was only seven and told me the Barracuda fish spiked him. Now he has confessed that he tore at his skin with fish hooks to get the radio inside his head to turn off. Am I to believe that all the fishing scars may have been self-inflicted? The rusty shark hook stuck through his hand was an accident though, surely. Or was it intentional?

Dearest Cynthia

Following our appointment in town yesterday, I popped into the newsagent and bought a thick red marker pen. It might be a crazy idea, but I am willing to try everything to keep Michael safe. This morning he unbuttoned his pyjama coat and showed me the red pen slash lines across his stomach and chest. His arms were marked along the veins in bright red. It gave me a fright when I saw how many lines of red he had made. Obviously this is worrying, although it wasn't dangerous; the red pen is our safe, symbolic knife. The bold red marks look like blood and Michael says it is absolutely satisfying. We were able to wash the marks off this morning and whether right or wrong, I didn't mention it to the psychiatrist.

Actually, there is a lot to tell. What will happen if I say what I really want to say—if I make a decision which I feel is best at the time but am wrong—and Michael suffers and is put in hospital?

There is so much more than that, enough to keep me awake all night.

The psychiatrist is now seeing Michael every day. He was noticeably astonished when Michael handed him a thirty page printed and tabled journal. He says we are a very sweet little family. However, we are not out of hot water—the doctor still wants to admit Michael to begin ECT. We beg for time to consider at each appointment. The threat and terror increases and Michael is vomiting daily.

I don't know whom I can trust. Yesterday we had an opportunity to discuss all our fears openly. Michael is terrified of going to hospital. The psychiatrist is allowing him two weeks on a higher dose of Risperidone and Luvox. He has also increased the Valium to reduce Michael's distress. I am hoping to be able to absorb and get used to what is going on. It is going to take some time to get a final diagnosis which will pick up the threads of other symptoms, the eating disorder, and OCD. The doctor tells us that Michael's situation is very serious and that ECT is not a vague option but is called for immediately. If this isn't terrifying enough, the psychiatrist now wants Michael admitted to the psych ward for perhaps several months. No, I cannot do that—I cannot commit my son to a mental hospital.

Fondly
Brigid

I was in an almost constant state of vague bewilderment. My doctor said it was anxiety based and that with all that was going on it wasn't surprising. I felt like I was living safely inside a thick glass bottle. I couldn't make this come right. No amount of great presents, videos, sweets—nothing could magically make this be not true. Sometimes love is not enough.

Never in my life had I been to so many appointments. After seeing the psychiatrist at the clinic we got into the lift and I said "Wow," because I thought I was looking at Russell Crowe. I said to the man, "I thought you were Russell Crowe!" He looked really amazed. The lift was tiny and we were quite squashed together. I said, "We just came from the psych floor." His eyes opened wide. We walked out to the carpark with him and funnily, we were parked next to each other. Standing in the warm sunshine, I felt calm and apologised for seeming odd. "You really do look like Russell, though," I added and waved as he drove off. The drive home through the forest was always enjoyable and stopping at the stall on the roadside, I left money in the honesty box for ten bunches of daffodils—enough to fill the whole house with a golden glow.

Hello dearest Cynthia

The days are getting longer; it is still light at 6pm. We are doing OK, though I can't help wondering what will happen next. It has been confirmed—Michael is autistic. I am aching all over today. The psychiatrist wants to know what is available regarding autism treatment and support in Tasmania. Why doesn't he know? Where do I begin? I wonder if there are any parents with adult autistic children at home? Would I be able to meet them? I need relevant books about autism. I will search the library online. I have so much new stuff inside my head that it throbs.

With love
Brigid

Autism seems to be an ambiguous disability. Many children with autism look normal. Some children are classically beautiful. Unusual skills can hide delayed development and communication problems. This was all very puzzling. I felt that the fault lay with me. I didn't know something was wrong with Michael and I blamed myself for it. Autism is a lifelong handicap. When I read this for the first time, it came as a terrible shock. How could life go back to normal now—whatever normal was? Michael remained the same—his personality and idiosyncrasies unchanged. Everything that is special and different about him is called "autism". It is hard to feel good about it.

Dear Cynthia

I just wanted to tell you that I'm sorry for freaking out. All the medical information has been a bit much. The psychiatrist doesn't know much about autism. He is going to find out about government funding that *will allow us to send Michael to Melbourne for specialist evaluation. The cost for a young child is $3,000. I don't know how much it costs for an adult—a lot more I suppose. The kettle is whistling and I am looking forward to a cup of strong, milky, sweet tea.*

With love
Brigid

Dear Cynthia

I want to share my good news with you. I found the phone number for a support group for parents with autistic children. I spoke with a lovely woman called Rose. There is a meeting next week. If Michael is calm enough to leave alone, Amelia-Jane and I will attend the luncheon. Rose wasn't shocked that Michael slept in a cardboard box when he was little. I was surprised that she wasn't shocked. A few days ago Michael asked me to get him a cardboard box to sleep in, a tunnelled home far from the world and light, somewhere he could protect himself from everything outside. Thinking we couldn't get one big enough, Amelia-Jane had a great idea. She is going to staple upholstery hessian on the walls of my room. It's the smallest room in the cottage, with one tiny paned window. We can move Mike's king-sized bed in there and Amelia-Jane and I will have a girls' dormitory in his big room. It'll be fun! We are spending tomorrow at home. I hope it will be as sunny as today is.

xxx Brigid

Amelia-Jane and I had a lovely time meeting everyone at the autism support group luncheon in the seaside village of Penguin. I was surprised to recognise several mums from the primary school Michael went to. On the way home I spotted an army Land Rover on the footpath outside a car yard. We stopped and I bought it for Mike. I was not a millionaire yet. Amelia-Jane would have to get two jobs to pay off my credit card. The "beast" cost $1000 and we could have made a good profit because, while we were paying, two blokes nearby were digging into their pockets for their wallets. The dealer suggested we resell it there and then, but I really wanted it for Mike.

Cynthia

I wonder if you mind me chatting about my fears? I have so many. Michael is much calmer and more settled in himself. We have an appointment this afternoon with the psychiatrist. He will undoubtedly ask me for my history report on Michael's development. Should I be open with him and say I have written it? I have reservations about sharing personal information with him. Having said that, Amelia-Jane and I have discussed the futility of the appointments if Michael and I are going to be secretive. I do understand the gravity of Michael's health and I am aware that mental illness is a serious and complicated malady. I do not trust the process. I feel that if Michael confided the full description of his experience for the last eight months, he might be diagnosed with something dreadful like schizophrenia. Michael wants to be honest, but is terrified of the outcome with a doctor keen to begin ECT. I am scared of losing control of the situation. I feel very bad about not realising that Michael is autistic. I always looked upon him as perfect and I still do.

Michael is terrified that he will be locked up. The duty doctor at the clinic warned me that should the psychiatrist decide Michael needs hospitalisation, the police will handcuff Mike and deliver him to the hospital psychiatric ward. The clinic is very near the police station; I estimate we would have maybe three minutes from the time of the phone call to escape. I want to share with you the extent of our terror, Cynthia. As a family, we have put into place a getaway plan of such intricacy that you may be forgiven for thinking we are in a war zone. We are very scared and the treatment is intensely distressing.

Regards
Brigid

I made a brief appearance at the carers group luncheon. I wasn't able to stay long because we had come from a very tiring appointment with the psychiatrist. Amelia-Jane had taken a very sullen Michael to the hospital pharmacy to pick up his medication. Everyone at the luncheon looked serene, sort of mystical. I felt bright red and wound up like a spring about to snap. I wondered if it would be fair of me to join this group of tranquil souls.

Dear Cynthia

Today the psychiatrist seemed amazed that I had doubts about Michael being autistic. The uncertainty was more of a wild hope, really. I also mentioned that I haven't been getting much sleep. Michael is up and down maybe six times a night and often wakes me at about 2am for a cuddle, because he's frightened. The psychiatrist looked astonished, "And you do this?" "Of course," I answered. "Wouldn't anyone?" I really do not mind that I feel constantly tired. I'm sad to say that my entire family has abandoned us. The psychiatrist said quietly, "It happens." He said he will not force Michael into hospital if we get some organised support for ourselves. Michael is about to have six sessions with a psychologist. I hope he and Michael will get on well.

The garden is full of daffodils, snowdrops and hyacinths. Michael is unable to do any task other than feed himself and his speech is scrambled. I am hoping that with the immediate threat of the psych ward and ECT on hold for the time being, he will relax a bit. I desperately need to share my fears and overwhelming confusion. My love for Michael might be clouding my judgement. This worries me and I have not found a qualified person with whom I can discuss my fears openly. The medical and fringe professional worlds seem divided in their views and goals about mental health.

With fondest love
Brigid

It was after 6pm and I'd been awake since 2am; I was weary and the day seemed to go slowly. I struggled to find words for how I felt. I'd never had emotions of this sort before. Around 2am I woke to find Michael standing at the end of my bed. He said he wanted to tell me something but felt frightened and needed a cuddle. As I held him gently he began to rock and became hot and sweaty. The rocking became increasingly rhythmic, almost violent. Michael told me he'd been protecting me from getting upset, but his strength was so depleted that he couldn't manage any longer. He said his brothers, Sam and Timmy physically and sexually abused and hurt him throughout his life and his older sister Tara knew. The rocking suddenly stopped, his pyjamas were soaked with perspiration and his hair was glued to the pillowcase with tears. It was four o'clock in the morning. I stood perfectly still with my feet pressed tightly together; waves of tearful terror flooded my body as I squeezed my eyes open and shut in an effort to understand what had just happened.

Very little sleep and lots of horrible shock had me spinning out and at 8am I felt floaty and calm, soft and safe and powdery blue. It felt wonderful. It didn't last long before a torrential flood of inner rage flooded my imagination with dark red and black. Edgar Allan Poe looked lame in comparison. I was alright and for the present would do nothing about revenge.

Amelia-Jane started working out a new last name for herself and I considered changing my name, too. Perhaps this was a little irrational, but what else could I do? The abuse seems to have happened during the day while I was home and the youngsters were playing. I read that sibling abuse results from a lack of parental supervision and care-giving responsibilities from older siblings. I believed I had a lovely little family when the children were younger, but now the happy memories are shattered by this heinous discovery. We had an appointment at the Sexual Assault Clinic for the following Wednesday.

I resolved to disengage from my entire family forever. I can't imagine what happened to my children to make them so violent and evil. I felt it was my fault and that confused me. People had always praised my fair and loving mothering and my children's lovely manners and behaviour. I wondered what I missed and felt desolate. Amelia-Jane was very low in spirit and horrified at being related to her sister and older brothers. Memories troubled me. Sam was abducted from our front garden when he was just four years old. He was found in a car with a man, who let Sam out and took off. After hours of police questioning my little boy, nothing useful was discovered and the case was closed. I never knew what happened during the time Sam went missing.

I had been to so many appointments during the past few weeks that my head felt ready to burst. I was weary, but matters were getting sorted. I was receiving a carer's payment from Centrelink and Amelia-Jane was studying a full-time Business Management Certificate. The tutor kindly allowed her to do the entire course from home. We needed to get her car repaired in time for her to return to work at the carrot factory the following month. There was nothing wrong with the little car mechanically, but the body was quite rusty. Our mechanic warned that the police could defect the car if they saw it on the road.

We met with the Centrelink psychologist last Thursday; he confirmed Michael was autistic but believed he also suffered from schizophrenia. That was a shock; I wanted to argue but knew he was just trying to help, so I said nothing. He recommended that the department grant Michael a Disability Pension. I had no expectations and, too tired to ponder, didn't mind either way.

Around lunchtime the next day, a suspicious parcel arrived with Michael's name on it. It was wrapped in stiff brown paper, tied with thick string and postmarked "Russian Federation." It was the complete current issue of "Sniper Wet Weather Gear". We each got an original WW2 KGB army backpack tied up with the oldest piece of string I'd ever seen. The backpacks cost $9 each. There is an abandoned warehouse in Moscow full of old war stuff and an astute Russian was selling everything on the Internet. Michael was delighted with his suit and KGB backpack. He called me his "precious little mother."

Michael and Anatoli

K-PAX, a movie starring Kevin Spacey, is about Prot, a patient at a mental hospital who claims to be from a distant planet and who has arrived on earth by means of "light travel." Prot displays puzzling knowledge and considerable influence over the other patients, promising to take someone with him upon his return to K-Pax on a set date. The next morning Prot is found lying catatonic under his bed.

"Star People" are believed to be extraterrestrial souls that have incarnated to fulfil a special mission here on earth. "Walk ins" allegedly enter our world through doorways between parallel dimensions, using soul transference to inhabit the physical body belonging to a living person who gives their consent. These subjects interest me now that Michael explained where he is originally from. He remembered how he came to be in baby Michael's body. He described his arrival from the source till his birth in so much detail that I easily pictured it as he spoke. Michael told me that my little baby's soul exchanged places with him during the delivery. A flood of grief made me cry as he continued to explain the reason he is here and what he needs to achieve. He believes he was sent to me to learn about relationships. I can imagine just a little how Mary felt when her Son, Jesus, as a young man realised his mission. Michael was named after the archangel who protects and helps fight off psychic attack. He offers strength and courage to get through the darkest days and inspires those who call on him, filling them with hope and faith. I desperately needed some of that hope.

One night Michael came out of his room and asked if I could sit with him; he had something important to tell me. I must have looked alarmed, Michael said it was nothing bad and not to worry. He held my hand in his and told me he was leaving and wanted to say goodbye. He picked up Amelia-Jane's guitar and strummed while singing a song he wrote for me. He'd never played guitar before. It was overwhelming. The words of his song opened my heart to an abundance of love and connection. I asked Michael if he would be gone by morning. He kissed my cheek gently, replying he had told me the things he needed to tell me and now many confusing situations had been clarified. It was done and, tired of this world, he needed to retreat. I wondered if I had my very own Star Man.

Afraid to go to sleep, I listened for Michael's car to start in the darkness. I woke extra early; the car was still in the yard—he hadn't left. I was so relieved. I baked a tray of jam tarts and hung out the washing before taking in his breakfast tray. Michael was still in his room, not moving—an empty human shell. My heart ached and prickled. This was too hard, too sad. I couldn't stop weeping. He said he'd be gone by morning and just like Prot he left on a moonbeam of light. How different he looked, like a house with the tenants gone and the electricity disconnected. I sat for hours in a deep, unfathomable state of loss, with Michael cradled in my arms, not responding to my touch or words.

I felt bleary. I'd been cuddling Mike since 2am. At about 4am Amelia-Jane got up and we stood at the end of Mike's bed singing his poems in different styles, including Bob Dylan, Leonard Cohen, Bette Middler and Nick Cave. I think my Jethro Tull version of Michael's "Ticks and Serpents" was the highlight. We made a huge racket and the dogs howled to get up.

Ticks and Serpents

The tick that I have previously seen,
Lives in a place that I have never been,
it lives in a place of mechanical creatures,
Weapons are among their many features.

The serpent I have seen in the past,
Slices through water so darn fast,
It has fluero yellow spots on its skin,
And also yellow zigzags on each fin.

Both these creatures are quite deadly,
Avoid them both when un-needly,
for if you are attacked by them too,
it will sure be the end of you.

Michael was 19 when he started drawing pictures of the creatures that had frightened him since he was a small boy. He first saw the Tick and the Serpent when he was in his early teens.

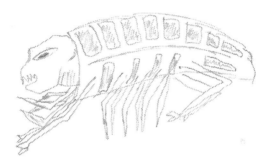

The Tick

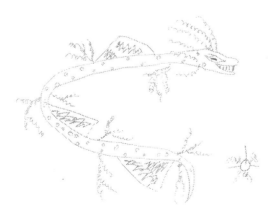

The Serpent

In the early morning mist I walked to the top of the hill. I walked fast and faster, then ran very fast. I wished that I could run fast enough to run past myself, turn around and meet myself running up the road and in that moment, make everything right again.

Dearest Cynthia

Thank you for not abandoning me. It has been snowing for two days and three nights. Everything is fresh and pure and hidden. Michael is very ill with bronchitis but otherwise quite calm. He says he has no real thoughts of suicide and no longer feels the need to cut or burn. The little he did caused no damage and little scarring. He is still writing in three journals and has twenty-eight poems, five songs and several stories.

I was pretty nuts when I wrote you those e-mails but since then I have had a session with a lovely man at Relationships Australia. I have another session with him next week. Everyone is being so kind and suitably horrified for little Mike. Michael is my treasure and he is no bother at all but is worried he is upsetting me. Well of course I am upset but we are doing ok. Amelia-Jane is a blessing all the time. We have two appointments this month in Launceston. Michael is seeing the colon-rectal surgeon. Although his wound has healed he is in great discomfort. So busy, busy, busy!

I am amazed at how much snow there is. The road to the west coast is closed and we are snowed in. The dogs love the snow and wag their tails all the time. It's cold, so I'm going to make a hot water-bottle to cuddle. I found out how to send hugs and kisses by computer. It's called a virtual hug.

With love
Brigid

Cold, blustery weather made being outdoors unpleasant, so we snuggled up to watch DVDs. Michael, however, said that he couldn't come out of his cardboard box—his room. I finished some very useful sessions with another psychologist, who believes I am doing well and that everything will be fine.

I learned a lot about families and how they function. The psychologist was concerned that I would get hooked back into all the family intrigue, but recognised a major shift in me and suggested that maybe I have managed to clamber out of the sewer.

I understood better what it's like to be Michael after watching the new release Stephen King movie *Riding the Bullet*. It depicts Michael and all his nightmares almost in sequence. We were amazed. I wondered if I should write to Mr King. Michael was confronted and deeply distressed to see his nightmares on the screen. He said as a young lad he'd often split into two and didn't know which was the real him; this bothered him, so he decided to embrace it and hoped to be able to train the split self to move further and further away from the self left behind, in order to spy.

Hi Cynthia

It's been a weird journey for the past five weeks. Is that all it's been? Five weeks? Thank you for standing by me through it all. The psychiatrist is pretty certain that Michael does not have schizophrenia. Thanks to the Risperidone the voices have stopped. Michael now tells me he is very lonely and wants the voices back. What? That made me blink. The psychiatrist says that Michael needs a huge amount of help to overcome his life experiences. It's very complicated. It seems 100% likely that Michael has always been autistic. So, dearest friend, our life is returning to normal. Well, our kind of normal anyway.

XXX Brigid

Michael showed me a drawing in his journal, a detailed egg shaped spaceship. When Michael was three and a half he had a vivid dream. A silver spaceship landed on the riverbank and tiny, soft people took him out of bed and then the house blew up. I told him that wouldn't happen and a week later the house burnt down. Was it premonition? He told me he heard them talking. Who was talking?

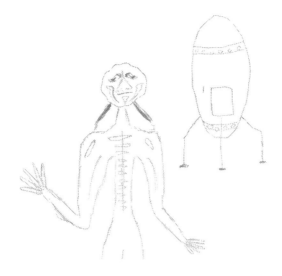

The Alien and the Space-ship

Dear Cynthia

I had another appointment with the psychologist earlier today. I asked him why the older children would have wanted to hurt their little brother. He believes they were jealous. Jealous! Oh Cynthia, what is happening? I can't believe this. Tara was 12 when Michael was born and yes she was terribly upset that her friends would see my bump as she called it. In fact she went berserk one morning and said she didn't want me picking her up from netball. Sam is 14 months younger than Tara. Both kids seemed to genuinely adore Michael when he was born. I shared with the psychologist some of the accidents Michael had as a toddler. Thinking back, it worries me to know that Sam was always involved. Why didn't I realise? Sam often took Michael down to the river. Isn't that just being a good big brother? So this tragedy is the result of my misplaced trust? What can I do about my rage? I want to bash my head against a wall.

One Christmas while holidaying at my parents, mum and I walked into the lounge and screamed. Sam was holding Timmy up in the air by his neck. After a quiet discussion with my parents, I decided to leave Timmy with them for a while, a decision which quite possibly saved his life, because a few months later the house burnt down. Timmy's room would have been engulfed in flames before the smoke reached my bedroom, waking me.

Sam became increasingly moody and angry. Perhaps this was because he no longer had his younger brother to bully. Amelia-Jane begged me not to leave her home alone with him. She sobbed, her soft brown eyes full of terror. In that moment I realised that things had to change immediately and they did. Every good thing I believed about my kids as a family was gone in that moment. I sought medical and legal advice and sixteen year old Sam was sent to his Egyptian father.

Dearest friend, what must you think of me? It cannot be worse than what I think of myself.

Fondly
Brigid

Michael was unwell; he had another ear and chest infection. The doctor referred him to an Ear, Nose and Throat specialist, who referred him to a dermatologist for systemic acne treatment. There were pustules inside his ear canals and we wondered if this might be connected to the Pilonidal abscesses. The specialist, doctor and chemist were amazed that I had let him play in the snow, given how sick he was. I believed the fun outweighed the harm. Michael was keen to get dressed and go outside to throw snowballs at his sister. The snow was deep and it was fun trying to walk across the yard. We took the boogie-boards into a grassy paddock and slid squealing down the hill between the amazed cows. Michael appeared happy and playful. I smiled.

The psychologist phoned to discuss appointment times. As part of the funded project—Better Outcomes for Mental Health—a doctor's referral allowed Michael six free sessions. Another family appointment with the hospital psychiatrist at the outpatients clinic heightened Michael's terror of being put in hospital for ECT. His dread clouded each visit, making the time pure misery. I was floundering. I didn't know who I could trust. Mum became increasingly annoyed with me and told me I was being silly. She didn't understand why we were so afraid of the psychiatrist. I was desperate to figure out what was happening, scared to go to sleep in case Michael did something unexpectedly dreadful. I wrote to my brother, but there was no reply. My uncle suggested I was being overly mothering. I was surprised at his interest; certainly he meant well, but cautioned me about the danger of involving my son with any psychiatrist. Baffled and lonely, I yearned for a hug.

The following week. I realised the bliss of being in shock; at least then everything is a hollow blur, although the feeling is lousy. The numbness wore off and exposed reality with a sickening thud. I was faced with getting on with practical daily tasks while my heart was breaking. I was grateful that until now the medical and family support had cost nothing. Our only expenses were petrol, pizza and videos. Petrol sky-rocketed to $1.30 a litre, such that the drive to Launceston appointments cost $70 return.

Several holiday auctions ended on e-Bay, including sixteen days in Florida, Mexico and the Bahamas. One sold for $5.50. Months passed since I'd won a $10,000 family holiday package to the Bahamas, Cancun, Florida and Las Vegas, with twenty-eight days of resort pampering, food and drinks included. I'd put together a colourful portfolio complete with maps and an itinerary of more than enough activity to satisfy even the most zealous tourist. Dolly Parton's Dixie Stampede in Orlando was at the top of the list, followed by Congo River Adventure mini-golf. Clearly, we wouldn't be ready to travel overseas any time soon. Biting my lip, I gave the tickets to the car salesman who sold me the Army Land Rover. His family were thrilled. Crazy about mini-golf, I added "world golf parks" to my wish list.

Dear Cynthia

You have been a great source of sensible help and a good friend. I spoke to a private psychologist earlier this week. He suggested that the things Michael is saying may just be psychosis and not fact. How will I know which it is? Also, after researching psychiatrists, we really need to stay with the Indian doctor for several reasons. Our family doctor gave me the phone number for a child psychiatrist in Launceston. I rang. He was surprised that I had his private number, as he no longer practices. That is because he was charged with sexually abusing young patients. Gosh—it's all a bit much, isn't it?

Mike thinks he is being a bother and upsetting me, but I thanked him for his disclosure. I'm done with Christians, or religious zealots

*of any kind. I'm done with my favourite relative and uncle. I'm done
with my mum; no more flowers, chocolates, sweet cards and letters.
I'm done with researching autism. I am not confused. I understand
things as they truly are and I'm not afraid. I was sobbing in bed last
night and said to Amelia-Jane, "I wonder what it will be like having
no family?" She replied, "Much the same, without all the upset."*

*I have a busy week with medical appointments. My tears have stopped
and I feel very acknowledged by you and everyone else involved. I will
keep in touch and maybe you noticed the omission of three names
from my done list. More on that later, Cynthia.*

*With fondest love
Brigid*

Michael had Launceston appointments with the colon-rectal surgeon,
the dermatologist and a psychiatric consultant from Sydney, all in a two
week period.

I was fortunate to get an appointment with the Sydney consultant on his
next visit to Launceston. I spoke with the receptionist, who asked how long
I'd known Michael was autistic. I replied, "Only a few months." She asked
what I had thought he was. "Perfect," I whispered.

Meanwhile at home, our bar fridge only stored a few bottles of milk
and ice cubes. Amelia-Jane and I drove to the coast and chose a brand new
refrigerator from the electrical store. We filled it with every delightful
comfort food imaginable, confident we were fully prepared for the busy
month ahead. Two days later the thermostat burnt out and the food went
rotten. The insurance paid for the replacement of the groceries and fridge,
but the setback was bitterly disappointing.

The blustery weather turned stormy; howling wind rattled loose sheets
of tin on the roof. Michael became increasingly glum. An hour before our
usual weekly appointment I telephoned and cancelled. I didn't like driving in
such weather. The Indian psychiatrist kindly faxed the script through to the
hospital pharmacy and Amelia-Jane picked the meds up the next morning.
Michael curled up in his reclining chair by the fire while we watched the film
Man of La Mancha starring Peter O'Toole and the beautiful Sophia Loren.

Michael liked the delusional character of Don Quixote very much. On
the plains of Spain, a country gentleman, Alfonso Quejana, imagines he is a

knight having many fantastic battles with other knights, beasts, giants and magicians, always winning the beautiful maiden in the end. His delusion deepens and Alfonso adopts the name of Don Quixote de la Mancha. Wearing his grandfather's suit of armour, he mounts an old horse and wanders the countryside with his companion Sancho Panza. Experiencing hallucinatory adventures, he suffers humiliation in a battle with a pair of windmills he perceives to be giants. The townspeople threaten and force Don Quixote to come to his senses and return home. He does, and in due course renounces his delusions as madness. Declaring his absurd heroism was nothing more than illusion, and that Dulcïnea was not the most desirable woman in the world but merely a whore, he dies from a broken heart. Amelia-Jane and I couldn't stop singing the songs and ordered the complete piano/vocal book from Amazon.

The following week our appointment with the Indian psychiatrist was rescheduled; he had flown back to India to assist the tsunami victims, returning to Tasmania around the end of December. The counsellor from the Carers Association came to the house. Impressed with my twenty-five page history report which I titled "Life with Mikey," he encouraged me to share it with the Sydney psychiatric consultant during our initial visit.

Things went haywire over the weekend. Michael suffered ten Jacksonian seizures in forty minutes and was rushed by ambulance to the Regional Hospital. During the seizure one remains conscious of everything, while completely and rigidly paralysed for several minutes at a time. It was horrible to watch dear Michael trapped inside himself. He was terrified of being left alone in the emergency cubicle so I sat with him for twelve hours of monitored observation. I hadn't slept in thirty hours by the time the specialist arrived to see us. Michael was admitted to a medical ward prior to EEG and CT scans. It was close to impossible for him to lie still; he trembled and jiggled violently. The staff became gentle and understanding when they were told of his autism and he was discharged following an in-depth discussion with the consulting neurologist. Dejected and troubled, I drove us both home.

Dearest Cynthia

I have news. Yesterday we drove to Launceston to meet with the Sydney consultant. Tears streamed down my face. The diagnosis is autism and early childhood onset of schizophrenia. How severe the autism is can't be decided due to the symptoms of schizophrenia. The consultant asked me why I was crying and I whimpered something about being sad. He agreed there is a lot to be sad about. He has increased Michael's Risperidone dose and added Tegretol to help with the tremors and Propanolol for anxiety.

I felt addled and woozy, my stomach twisted into a tight knot. We left the consulting suite, carefully navigating the narrow stairs. Outside in the daylight the hustle and bustle of a city street seemed a little unreal, like coming out of a cinema into the afternoon sunshine. We walked slowly towards the carpark, past a store that sells camping gear and all sorts of fascinating hardware. I suggested we each buy something appropriately symbolic. Michael went straight to the knife cabinet. In that moment I said, "Choose whichever you wish." Am I ridiculously foolish? Was it such a crazy thing? I think the knife is a symbol of trust. What if I'm wrong Cynthia? What if I'm wrong?

Running to a public toilet, my body seemed to take on a life of its own. My bowels exploded, bile rose up into my throat; my head pounded so hard I thought I was going blind. I stuffed thick wads of paper towel between my legs in hope of not soiling the car. It was a long drive back to the mountains. Amelia-Jane pulled off the highway many times. My whole being turned inside out.

This afternoon is sunny and warm, a perfect day really. Michael is still asleep. It seems that yesterday was just a bad dream. Michael can't have schizophrenia.

XXX Brigid

Amelia-Jane and I stood in the garden sipping tea, enjoying the sunshine and cool breeze. Michael stiffened, staring at the ground where a hole opened up like a miniature volcano and thousands of big black ants spurted out. He just stood there staring at them crawling across his boots and up his legs. Amelia-Jane and I couldn't see them. Michael was hallucinating.

Michael refused to eat; he was distressed and talked of killing himself as he fluctuated between being passive and boisterous. I looped out and tried to bang the back door off its hinges. Outside in the garden I hurled my mug into the tree, splashing coffee over myself.

The Sydney consultant told me not to speak with my mother on the phone, concerned that her lack of understanding and criticism of the general situation was detrimental. There was so much meanness in my family and I wondered how we would get past Mikey's terrible sadness. I wondered if my rage, pain and despair would be a turning point. The shock and mourning over the diagnosis continued but in spite of my turbulent feelings, I still had to cope with everyday needs. Fear of failing to care for Michael and keep him safe caused me to have a total loss of confidence in my abilities. Psychiatrists were telling me how my child thinks and what he should or should not do, and how he feels. Over the past twelve months I had been constantly torn between hope and despair. I was tired, angry and very frightened. Cynthia alone understood the depth of my unhappiness.

Darling Cynthia

Amelia-Jane and I settled Michael in bed and drove to town yesterday for groceries. He was still asleep when we returned. This afternoon Tara phoned and asked if Michael was OK, then went on to say she was very worried he might have killed himself yesterday. Panic rose up inside me. Why would she think such a thing? Apparently she drove up to the house yesterday while we were in town. Michael answered the door. She told him that she and her brothers couldn't be friends with him if he lived with me. I am horrified, Cynthia. What does she mean? Amelia-Jane is amazed at the timing of Tara's arrival. It's all very strange. Tara lives an hour's drive away; we were only gone for two hours. It is alarming that she thought her conversation with Michael might have pushed him to commit suicide. I recently confronted her about the childhood bullying and abuse. Trembling and visibly shaken, she denied knowing anything—though her initial gasp included a comment about the boys doing something to Michael.

XXX Brigid

I opened the back door to get an armful of wood and squealed. Dark brown spiders were running over the door and outside walls—Tasmanian wolf spiders about the size of a man's thumbnail. I wondered if I imagined them, but they were real. The wolf spider is a roving nocturnal hunter with three rows of eyes. Preying on other spiders, grasshoppers, crickets and even small mice, they are ground dwellers, living in silk-lined burrows in soft earth. Michael bravely stood out on the back step with the torch and squished ninety-seven of them. I mentioned the midnight excitement to our neighbour, who was amazed. It was very strange.

Things were getting rather weird. Michael was frightened of the men in his room. Crouched each side of the bed, they discussed his behaviour and the punishments they would inflict on him. A few nights in a row, Michael stared at the bedroom wall. He looked terribly ill. I asked what he was looking at; he described a brutal attack on a young girl. A small hole appeared in the wall and grew as he watched; the wall peeled back in layers, allowing him to see into the next room where a man was beating the little girl. She was sobbing. The room filled with red light and smoke. Michael worried about the little girl. I worried about Michael.

I was disappointed that the new psychologist in whom I had placed all my hope, refused to see us as a family. Preferring to see Michael alone, he told him he had never been autistic, was definitely not schizophrenic and that the seizures were caused by the antipsychotic medication. I was aware that autism can change physical reactions to some drugs, but there were other things to consider, like terror and self-harm.

On New Year's Day in the late afternoon, Michael's dog attacked him, biting into his leg. Michael needed to be seen by a doctor and given a tetanus shot and broad spectrum antibiotics for possible infection. Surprisingly, the wound didn't need stitching. We had never met the doctor before; he was on call for the holidays. While chatting together, he told us he was at the Isle of Wight concert back in the late 60's. Amelia-Jane told him we had a video of that amazing concert but had never met anyone who was actually there in the mud and slush.

The doctor's room was opposite the supermarket. We walked over to buy a treat for supper. There were only a few cars in the carpark; we joked about what sort of people go to the supermarket on the first night of the year. Choosing strawberries, Michael pointed. I looked, then grabbed the end of the trolley and ran down to the meat fridges with Amelia-Jane still holding the handle. The Indian psychiatrist from the local hospital outpatient clinic happened to be in the supermarket at the same time as us and I didn't want him to see me. In October we had secretly begun the $165 appointments in Launceston with the Sydney psychiatric consultant and expressed our fear of hospital treatments. The consultant sent a copy of his diagnosis and full report to the Indian psychiatrist and by now he'd have read it. If we had been open and truthful in the beginning, what would have happened to Michael? I shuddered to think about that.

Although the Indian psychiatrist was kind, his peculiar use of English, wrinkled clothes, greasy hair, grubby fingernails and general appearance of needing a hot soapy bath did not gain our trust; neither did the ever present threat of the hospital psych-ward. We told our family doctor we could never go back and she agreed. I rang to cancel all future appointments and the conscientious receptionist insisted on knowing why. I panicked and lied that we were moving interstate.

Back in the supermarket, Amelia-Jane suggested in the shampoo aisle that maybe I was overreacting. She suggested we just say hello to the Indian psychiatrist. Of course she didn't know about the lies I told. We were still arguing when he came down the aisle and off we ran again. Michael, ill with pain from the bite on his leg, took the car keys; limping through the glass doors into the night, he looked like a man escaping a hostage situation. There were only six people in the supermarket, including the three of us, so there was not much chance of blending into the crowd. The Indian psychiatrist got to the checkout at the same time as us. Amelia-Jane, quite cross with me for being ridiculous, was nearly wetting herself with stifled laughter.

After the dog bit Michael I telephoned the vet, who asked to examine Anatoli in the surgery the next morning. For nearly a month Anatoli coughed, refused to get out of bed—sometimes for a day or more—but ate well. He had always been a tired puppy and absolutely intolerant of exercise. I didn't know how sick Anatoli was; the vet said he was born with a faulty heart valve, which is why he never wanted to play, walk far or get out of bed. I understood that the dog was unwell but not why he would deliberately bite Michael from behind. The vet warned that treatment at this stage would be hit and miss and recommended deep sleep euthanasia. Amelia-Jane and I held the dog in his last minutes. It was horrible. I paid the vet to bury him; neither Amelia-Jane nor I had the energy to dig a hole deep enough for a wolfhound.

Ronnie woofed and woofed. By 5am I couldn't stand any more and went across the road to see if a native animal was trapped in a fence. There on the step was, of all things, a puppy—an eight week old Queensland cattle dog. I love the smell of young pups. We spent a lovely morning playing with it, Michael curled up in bed while the puppy bounced all over him. That afternoon I drove to town and gave the puppy to the RSPCA. Michael heard a car slow down and idle out the front at about 1am. Perhaps someone had been given the puppy for Christmas and didn't like the crying and bother. Whatever the story behind the strange arrival, it made us laugh. 2006 was full of the unexpected.

In our next meeting with the Sydney consultant in Launceston, Michael was so much improved that the consultant used the word "miraculous." He was pleased and amazed with Michael's progress and with the beneficial changes we were making in our lives. He frowned, though he wasn't cross that we'd tapered off the meds and agreed that Michael didn't need any at present. The consultant felt that if we maintained a calm environment and lifestyle, Michael may well be able to get along without any medication at all. He patiently listened to the sad story of the dog's death; though questioned my somewhat bizarre behaviour in the supermarket at seeing the Indian psychiatrist. I confessed I was so worried about Michael's reaction to the loss of his Wolfhound, I sedated him with Clonazapam for two days. The consultant acknowledged my concern but said that sometimes people just need to feel upset. It was a relief to be truthful and understood.

The mining boom set in motion the opportunity for Amelia-Jane to step up to the challenge of becoming the first female underground driller in Australia. The Henty Gold Mine was 140kms across the mountains. Amelia-Jane back-packed at the Cecil Hotel in Zeehan, returning home for a few days every three weeks. My crushing loneliness was alleviated by her visits. We both loved the mountains and walked for miles exploring creeks, following Tasmanian Devil tracks and discovering hidden waterfalls. At home I pottered about in the garden, while Amelia-Jane sat under the Oriental Cherry tree, perfecting her favourite concerto for clarinet with CD backing by the Stuttgart Philharmonic Orchestra. It was delightful and I felt deeply content. The three days of each break whizzed by. With the household tasks done and enough wood split and stacked to last me for the next few weeks, Amelia-Jane packed the car and drove back over Mount Black to the west coast. Loneliness got a whole lot lonelier.

The past weeks had been nerve-wracking. Twenty minutes walk over the hill stood a cluster of houses built to accommodate the workers at the old potato station. In 1933 the station raised certified seed for Tasmania's potato industry. Boguns renting the houses were using the old gravel pit behind our barn as a dumping ground for car bodies. Sliding around the corner of our garden screeched three heavy-duty utes, each dragging an overturned car. The tow chains clanged as the cars slid and skidded like snakes on the road, spewing shattered glass and bits of rusty metal across the front lawn. The noise was deafening and I swept up glass and bolts for days.

Amelia-Jane and I walk past the gravel pit on our way to the lake; the smell was awful. Close to a hundred car bodies were piled up along with dented rusty washing machines, microwave ovens and filthy household rubbish spreading into the old growth forest.

The early Tasmanian explorer Henry Hellyer discovered velvet worms only fifteen kilometres from our property. It was sad that human wreckage was now encroaching on the habitat of ancient creatures, survivors from Gondwanaland considered to be the link between worms and jointed animals.

An orphan joey

Meanwhile, Michael's depression suddenly lifted and he became interesting to the point of unnerving. Going into trance at will, awake and conversational, he couldn't remember anything afterwards, so Amelia and I scribbled most of it down. We had been besieged with demons. Four had names and a compass direction. Michael documented detailed descriptions, names, missions and where they came from. Michael told me that while he was alone a demon named "Alteaz" attempted possession. The Catholic priest wanted Michael to recite a protection prayer but Mike refused. I asked if he would accept a guardian angel or gatekeeper and he agreed. Within minutes he came out of his room and handed me a drawing of a tall man with long blond hair and blue eyes, dressed in white silky trousers and a below-the-knee white coat with big shiny silver buttons. Whatever I expected, it wasn't that.

"His name is Alex," Michael said. "Alex is here now to answer questions."

Michael lay back on the recliner in the lounge room, shut his eyes and breathed so slowly that I wondered if he was breathing at all. Amelia-Jane and I glanced at each other with puzzled looks, wondering what we could ask.

Our cottage was built ninety-seven years ago by a young Mr Grinnell, for his bride. He cut the trees into timber and made his own nails. The deep well was dug using a tin cup while he dangled on a rope held by his friend. Amelia-Jane knew she had bought more than a hobby-farm; she had bought a piece of Tasmanian history and the few scattered neighbours in the area had plenty of tales to tell, some quite intriguing. The cottage had been in a terrible mess when Amelia-Jane bought it as a deceased estate. Although the elderly couple who'd lived there had been dead more than twenty years, their personal belongings and household furniture remained in place and local gossip hinted that the farm was haunted by Mr. Grinnell himself. I had a crazy hope that there was money or something of value buried in the garden. It was a good place to start with questions.

Me: "Does Mr Grinnell have a secret treasure?"
Alex: "Not sure."
Me: "Can you make him go to the light?"
Alex: "No, he doesn't want to leave."
Although the room was cosy and the wood fire crackling, the temperature dropped significantly. I shivered.
Alex: "Mr Grinnell is upset by Brigid's comment, but he likes her being here looking after things."
I apologised aloud, though I was unsure for what.
Amelia-Jane: "Is all the coming and going from the gravel-pit land creating a disturbance?"

> Alex: "Yes. Damazus is upset and Geoffrey came inside the cottage.
> The house is built on a vortex and other spirits will come—some
> will be unpleasant."
> Brigid: "Can we close the vortex?"
> Alex: "No."
> Amelia-Jane: "Should we leave?"
> Alex: "No. Mr Grinnell knows about the vortex. He doesn't want you
> to leave; not yet. He wants you to take the sheds down in the potato
> paddock. He's pleased the car shed is knocked down. Damazus has
> always been on this land. Nobody knew till now. Damazus is not
> happy about any of you walking through the bush. He is watching."
> Amelia-Jane: "Did people really live in the small huts in the paddock?"
> Alex: "Yes."

Michael stirred, opened his eyes, stood up and went back to bed. Amelia-Jane and I sat looking at each other. Outside the dogs barked and the weird atmosphere dispelled. It was very strange. We wondered who Geoffrey was.

Nights became congested in our tiny lounge room; the air was freezing cold and an overpowering smell of sweat and grime lingered. Alex informed us through Michael that this was the spirit of the potato labourer who lived in the hut in the paddock with his daughter, Julia; his name was Geoffrey King. A man raped Julia, a fight resulted and the man killed Geoffrey and buried his body in the forest near our barn. He does not want us to find his bones—he wants to haunt the forest around the house. The acreage has caused arguments and strife over the years. I endeavoured to validate the story, but the evidence I uncovered was flimsy at best. It was a scary experience walking in that forest. The owner gave us permission to do so, amazed that anyone would want to. Amelia-Jane and I had previously discussed purchasing the seventy acres but the owner was reluctant. In light of Alex and Michael's recent disclosure that the land had ghosts and a reigning demon, our disappointment became a light hearted sense of relief.

The marijuana smell that moved about was a spirit named Julie, a friend of Sam's lover Renee, who called herself the Princess of Darkness. Tara came to stay with us in 2003 and we all squashed into the beach cottage. I smelt dope around Tara, who insisted she didn't know why. At first the smell came from her purse and inside her van, then wafted freely. Spirit Julie claimed through Michael that the odour was her. Tara left the van with us for several months, then returned without warning and took it. At times the smell hung about in the middle of the road or around the well. Poor Julie was left at our house. She doesn't want to be helped or enlightened in any way; she just wants to find Tara.

Regarding the eye that Mike first saw while in the car at the supermarket car park when he was three: the eye's owner claims his name was Travis. He was killed in 1972 by a fat boy named Roger Tearny somewhere near Leigh Creek in the remote north of South Australia. Roger buried Travis in the desert. The boys, who had been childhood friends in Adelaide, were aged sixteen at the time. Travis first attached to my young son Timmy in Adelaide and when Michael was three attached to him, pretending to be his helper, companion and friend. He now claimed he did this to get Michael to hunt down Roger and kill him in revenge. When I encouraged Travis to look to the light, he became very hostile. I attempted to verify the murder, though short of speaking with the police, what could I do? I resolved to one day visit Leigh Creek in the outback of South Australia and maybe find historical evidence that a boy named Travis disappeared.

Michael shared with me the poem he wrote in his journal . . .

White Pupil Eye

I see this odd eye in my mind
Looking at it helps me unwind
It is not a normal round type eye
It has an appearance quite sly.

It has a pointy iris that is quite black,
The white is covered by many a red zigzag track
But as for the important fact, it will now enter
This eye has a small white pupil right in the centre.

The white pupil looks so living
It appears to be quite giving
Giving of dreams so intense and fearful
The dreams it gives are not at all cheerful.

Still this eye does persist
I don't mind that it does exist
This odd eye has long been a part of me
So when I see it I will never flee.

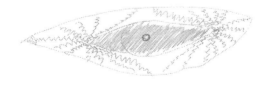

The gatekeeper Alex turned out to be a guardian with minimal ability, though he was pleasantly chatty. Michael requested another gatekeeper last night; a woman called Elfbet answered his call; she sits with eyes shut and hands clasped. He described her as round—she does not speak.

Michael wrote in his tabled journal everyday. He wrote poems, songs and documented the activity of the demons he believed were waiting to kill him . . .

The Four Evils

Karnacus of the West

The lying demon of Hell. He called himself "Lucifer." He was lying. He is really Karnacus. This demon is a liar and tries to trick you at everything. Karnacus is blood-lusting. He wants to see blood and lots of it. He waits until you are vulnerable and willing to show him what he wants. He wounds.

Lazarus of the East

Lazarus is a rotting, stinking demon. All he wants is to see you rot. He is constantly yelling it out of his big-toothed mouth. He has a big head with one very large eye aligned vertically. This eye has red veins running through it—caused by the strain of his constant yelling. He has a very big mouth with enormous goofy teeth. His body is rotting away and some parts can be seen through. You can see the bones in his body because he is so thin.

Damasus of the North

Damasus is an old hobbling demon. He watches for you to trip both physically and mentally. He follows at a distance watching and waiting for the chance to pounce. He wears gloves to cover his hands and big leather boots with bone buckles. He hides deep inside his cape. He hobbles along with a walking stick that taps. He is short but fast.

Arkanos of the South

This demon is a red-skinned, short and furious little fellow. He hides while your barrier is up, waiting to strike once you let it down. Then he strikes you with all his strength. Arkanos is very short with tight red skin covering his entire body. He wears no clothes. He is muscular and strong. His floppy ears sway as he moves his raging head. Steam comes out of his slitted, lumpy nose.

The Catholic priest was adamant that he needed to perform an exorcism. The idea seemed rather extreme, though I was worried about what seemed to be strong psychic attacks on Michael. At times he spoke in Latin. It was more than creepy. I couldn't help but wonder if I were in a Stephen King story, or an episode of *Charmed*. This was our reclusive life in the Tasmanian mountains.

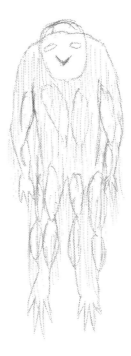

Lazarus of the East

Hi Cynthia

Michael is terribly ill again. I drove him to the Medical Centre this morning after a disturbed night. I only slept for two hours, so you can imagine how I look. The GP mentioned I wasn't my usual chatty, cheerful self. I am embarrassed to tell you I was rude. She was amazed and asked me what was wrong. What's wrong? Can you believe that? I went on and on about how tired I am every day. I sounded like a real whiner. She suggested I need to spend time with friends and go out for coffee and I burst into tears. She said I need more sleep. That is true. Michael wakes me up every night and I do feel worn out. Isn't sleep deprivation the fastest route to psychosis? Perhaps I should go to the carers meeting next month. I am struggling to understand schizophrenia. I am expecting to wake up one morning and find our life back to normal. I cannot keep living like this. Maybe it is time to let go and embrace this strange new way of life. If angels exist, then surely so do demons.

XXX Brigid

Dearest Cynthia

I am defeated. The months have slipped by and with them my hope. I no longer complain about the little things I miss. The intense loneliness I struggle to overcome, the terrible sadness that whelms up inside me daily and my gradual, but now complete withdrawal from social interaction are the realities I now endure. I have been absorbed into Michael's world and the past year has rendered me heart-broken and anxious. For the first time I cannot find any comic relief in a tragic situation.

Michael, Amelia-Jane and I came to believe that only through death would we be released from the endlessly deceptive, bewildering madness we endure. Is it always darkest before the dawn? At 4am this morning we sat together on the bed. Silently we began, our hands cupped. A simple plan Cynthia. All we had to do was swallow. Released from despair, the three of us drifted into deep sleep. I awoke feeling nauseous and dazed.

In the afternoon sunshine I felt an intense urge to phone the carers' freecall number. What a relief it was to hear someone's voice. I felt deeply ashamed to confess that my courage had failed. My perception was warped; I did not recognise reality for what it is. I listened to her words. Now I know that our idea was a horrid way to die, slow and very painful. I didn't want that. The warm sunshine on my back made me feel limp and calm and commonsense had returned.

My head aches, Cynthia, and my eyes are scratchy and swollen from weeping. The strain of our circumstances has depleted my energy and that is also true for Amelia-Jane. Sensible changes need to be made—that much is certain. I will take one step at a time and focus on practical goals to reduce our fear and worry. I will think about my previous behaviour, dear friend, and endeavour to laugh at my own seriousness. I am fully exhausted.

Fondly

Brigid

It was agreed. Amelia-Jane would sell the house and paddocks. An unusually enlivened Michael offered to walk little Ronnie. I guessed his sudden vitality was a good sign. Within the hour a man pulled up and said he wanted to buy Michael's Land Rover, which was still abandoned in the long grass. He returned the following day with cash and removed the vehicle. It was extraordinary that a dark blue car under a tree, in a paddock of long grass, scarcely visible, had been spotted by a motorist driving past on a mountain back road.

The following afternoon Amelia-Jane phoned from the Queenstown Hospital. Injured while underground in the mine, she was coming home for several months. Later that day an elated real estate agent phoned to say he had a firm buyer. Amelia-Jane, suffering shock and excruciating pain, refused the sale. He rang the next morning with three offers, each for more than the asking price. "Surely you have to choose one," he said—and she did.

Cars, furniture and possessions continued to sell with little effort and for dazzling amounts. No-one made near offers and the lady who bought my coupe urged me to accept more than the advertised price. Curiosity overcame me; something bewitching was happening. Michael had sprung to life since the cottage sold and people noticed the snap change in him. Two roadhouses in the area had been on the market for years. After we asked Michael to pray, the businesses sold immediately. I questioned Michael; he smiled and said, "It's a kind of magic."

We paid the credit card debt of $70,000. Amelia-Jane and I ruthlessly culled our personal belongings and found a good farm home for my little dog. Three weeks later, a truck arrived to move our packed boxes and beds to a storage container.

We'd endured four years of illness, surgeries and tormenting pain, psychiatric weirdness, demons and hallucinatory fiends, tears and loneliness. Now it was time to holiday. We rented a beach house on the east coast of Tasmania. Michael and I wandered over the sand dunes and rocky beach for hours each day, collecting shells. Michael photographed birds and rocks, white crested turquoise waves rolled onto the golden sand and delicate jellyfish washed up on the beach. Each day held the possibility of new discovery.

A storm brewing turned the sky black; the waves roared and smashed onto the reef. A hefty sea lion sat staring out to sea. I wondered if he were sick or injured. Before I could get close, he bounded at me barking. Squealing, I scampered up a sand hill and turned to see Michael sitting beside the creature with less than an arm's width between them. The magnificent animal was looking at Michael, who spoke to him for twenty or more minutes while taking photographs. The sea lion humped his way into the ocean and was gone. I was in awe of Michael—my very own Star Man—my special man from Atlantis with the Steve Irwin gene. I felt very silly for running away. Days later, a local fisherman told us to be careful of sea lions since someone had been savagely mauled by a big male.

During our holiday, Michael cleverly rewired the entire electrical system on Amelia-Jane's Renegade Jeep, using diagrams he downloaded off the internet. In celebration of new beginnings, she treated us to dinner at the beachfront restaurant; we were the only diners. The background music, candles and roar of the ocean were charming. Michael ordered a seafood platter and pulled a face at a raw oyster, poking it with his fork. Amelia-Jane and I grinned. Michael had never understood the value of money. When I'd ask him how much a chocolate bar cost, he'd reply "$50." "What about a lawnmower?" "$50" was his guess. Dinner was delicious and our mood elated. With only a few chips left on his plate, Michael toyed with the oyster. "I'll give you $50 if you swallow it," I teased. Michael bragged that he wasn't the sort of person who could be bought. "Everyone has a price Michael, even you," I said. I laughed, watching Michael stab at the oyster with his fork. "$100 if you swallow it," I dared him. He shook his head, pursing his lips. Amelia-Jane winked, "I'll give you $1000 if you swallow it." We'd found his price. Down slid the oyster. Michael turned a little green. We cheered. The waitress said we were mean. I watched my dessert slide off the plate in her hand onto the floor as she suppressed her laughter. The next morning we drove to a nearby town; Amelia-Jane went to an ATM and gave Michael his well deserved cash.

Dearest Cynthia

*I have a good feeling about our future. I believe as a family we have
made good decisions. Amelia-Jane's leg is almost healed and she
will return to work in the mine after Christmas. Michael and I are
confident that we can create a new life for ourselves in Adelaide. Wish
me well, dear friend.*

With fondest affection
Brigid

During three wonderful months on the east coast of Tasmania the
highlight was our walk to South Cape Bay. Two hours drive south of Hobart,
at the end of Australia's southernmost road is the Cockle Creek camping
area. From there it's an easy three hour walk through forest, across native
heaths, followed by a winding scrub track out onto the crumbling cliffs of
Australia's southern tip. Far below, monstrous four-metre waves collapsed
onto the sandy beach while we gazed across the vast cold blue Southern
Ocean, all that lay between us and Antarctica. Michael photographed the
board walks, tracks and ocean views but what I liked most was his obvious
eye for detail in the photos of plants. Unfortunately Michael's digital photos
were lost when his camera fell into the sea a few weeks later.

With only a few days of our incredible holiday left, we packed ready for
the new beginning in Adelaide. We drove to the ship; sailing from Devonport
across Bass Strait overnight, we arrived in Melbourne next morning and
headed to Adelaide along the Great Ocean Road. Adelaide is my hometown
and I was pleased to be back. Friends, now aware of Michael's diagnosis,
withdrew and ceased contact. That really hurt. I was disheartened; my
perceived rejection by family and friends left me more isolated and lonely
than I believed possible. The mining industry had taught Amelia-Jane to
believe in herself. She was a qualified underground diamond-core driller
now, with her own rig and off-sider. My heart swelled with pride at my
daughter's strength and determination. As the Aussie saying goes, it was
time to "eat a spoonful of cement and harden up."

Michael and I leased a gorgeous fully furnished Victorian mansion in
the vibrant café and restaurant hub of North Adelaide. Wide leafy streets
and the stunning architecture of grand old homes make it one of the best
places to live in Adelaide—if you can afford it. There are plenty of shops, a

cinema, all-day bakery and the entire suburb is surrounded by beautiful rose gardens and parklands; it exudes a village feel and has a pretty walk into the city centre across the river.

Michael had always worn his hair long and parted in the middle— the Sydney consultant had made particular reference to the "girlie" style. I indulged myself with tea and cupcakes, while Michael had his hair professionally styled. He strolled into the café with a Roger Federer haircut and a bag of styling products. My eyes filled with tears. On the bag were printed the words, "Dare—change is a matter of seeing things differently."

Change was the only constant in our lives and change we did. I joined Herbalife International, which was coincidentally celebrating its 25th Australian Anniversary in Adelaide that week. I met men and women who inspired and motivated me to believe in myself. Within weeks of settling into our new home Michael enrolled in a Tax Accountant Course. Although he did not continue after he went mentally blank in the first exam, ample tax tips made it worth the course money. Michael made a brave effort to speak with people using the telephone. He spoke clearly and with daily practise overcame his former speech difficulties. He made friends and contacts through a photography social club and a young entrepreneur business group.

The Aquatic Centre nearby ran a high-board diving class. Michael signed up and shaved his armpits, which made me giggle. He also joined a scuba diving team, went away with them on weekends and now has an Open Water qualification. It was amusing to see the way he'd drape his gear around the elegant bathroom; two huge black flippers and a pair of air tanks in the bath, a diving suit, gloves and goggles dangling from the shower rail. It looked like the man from Atlantis had shed his skin.

I had a free $1000 ticket to Empowernet, one of Asia Pacific's most successful promoters of professional and personal development programs. Amelia-Jane was flying over to Adelaide for her birthday—we had planned a girls' shopping weekend. I suggested to Michael that he attend the event. He had never been away from home alone but said he'd like to go. The travel agent arranged a pleasant hotel suite next to the Conference Centre in Melbourne and booked flights and taxi transport to and from the airports. Michael rang from the hotel to ask if he could use my credit card to purchase tickets to Anthony Robbins' "Unleash the Power Within" seminar. Later in the year, he and Amelia-Jane flew to Sydney to participate in a weekend event that changed their lives. Annihilating fear as they walked across a bed of hot coals, they knew for certain that there was nothing they could not overcome.

The move to Adelaide was an excellent choice; Michael liked the anonymity of a city lifestyle. We each bought an annual pass to the zoo. Michael enjoyed photographing the animals while I strolled along pathways sipping coffee. He joined a city gym for $80 a week and told me his personal trainer was very pretty. Through Empowernet Michael joined an online international trade group. I wasn't concerned about our extravagant everyday spending; Michael was doing well with the online trading each night. The Trade Company approached him about leading a support group for traders in Adelaide. My heart fluttered with joy as I watched him interacting with people from varied walks of life.

Late on a hot summer night, Michael walked to the bakery for a pie and upon his return proudly announced that he had sat down in the bakery to enjoy his first cup of coffee. Mike thrived in the city and looked stunning in his new clothes, $250 business shirts, silk tie, suit, sports jacket and layered designer outfits and for the first time in his life he wore jeans. Standing tall and strong, he was indeed an empire on legs.

Invited by the Trade Partners to attend a conference on Hamilton Island, Michael spent several days in Brisbane visiting Steve Irwin's Australia Zoo on the way. The portfolio of photographs and video clips he created was breathtaking. During the conference Michael was asked if he would like to fly to Chicago to spend time on the live trade floor with the team. Unfortunately, before the trip was arranged, the Global Financial Crisis shook our investments and we had to view the situation differently.

After completing courses in Reflexology and Reiki, I worked three days a week in the Adelaide Arcade. Michael secured a full time position as a Linux Server Administrator in a software company in the CBD. We gave up the mansion a few months later; Michael leased a city apartment and I returned to Tasmania to live and work in Zeehan. Glowing with optimism and renewed enthusiasm, I was glad to be alive. Looking back, I wondered how we got through all the weirdness and heartache.

I am thankful for the support and understanding I received from Carers Tasmania staff during those arduous years. I was grateful for the freecall service and often at night would phone just to feel connected. Knowing that someone would be there for me the next morning gave me the strength to hang on. Without this team of tireless supporters, Amelia-Jane, Michael and I would be dead. Friends were understandably bewildered and tired of the endless nightmarish drama. My sense of aloneness was unbearable. Unable to speak about how despairing I felt, I began e-mail with a new friend I created in cyberspace—"Cynthia." It was a relief to express myself fully to her, for she alone knew the depth of my grief.

Profoundly alone and completely stranded, Michael had been caught in an abyss between the old way of life and the new possibilities. Carl Jung wrote that when the soul embraces and accepts suffering, the pain reveals itself as the birth pangs of a new inner being. The four year journey into a macabre and surreal alternate reality could be likened to a grim fairytale. What amazed me most was the depth of intimacy and sense of belonging that Michael, his sister Amelia-Jane and I developed.

I have been asked why I didn't know Michael was autistic or unusual; after all, he was my fifth child. I wonder that, too. The consultant suggested I had become "habituated" and therefore did not view Michael's oddness as the wider community did. Whatever the reasons, my innocence ironically gave Michael the freedom he needed to develop into the confident and happy man he is today.

Afterword

Proceeds from the sale of this book will be used to fund an innovative residential crisis care program—based on the Temenos vision—for people in acute personal crises, including schizophrenia. This practical vision for genuine "mental health" reform will take the form of a homelike community network, which will provide family support as well as wholistic, humane, non-coercive and natural alternatives to drug-based psychiatry and hospitals for people in crisis. Staff and residents will work and share together through equal dialogue and there will be a focus on re-empowering therapies, good nutrition, caring relationships, communion with nature and teaching self-help skills.

Temenos is a Greek word which refers to a universal instinct to create an inner and/or outer safe space—akin to a garden, piece of sacred land, guarded castle, or womb—in which to heal, reorganize and regenerate the fragmented, depressed, or traumatised personality. The temenos is simultaneously created and protected by the caring community network.

Further reading: www.jungcircle.com/temenos.html